Webinars FOR DUMMIES

A Wiley Brand

by John Carucci
Sharat Sharan
Contributors:
Tricia Heinrich
Mark Bornstein
Mark Szelenyi

FOR DUMMIES
A Wiley Brand

Webinars For Dummies®

Authorized reprint by Wiley India Pvt. Ltd., 4435-36/7, Ansari Road, Daryaganj, New Delhi – 110002.

Published simultaneously in Canada

Reprint: 2015

Printed at: Delhi Press, Delhi.

ISBN: 978-81-265-5280-1

Contents at a Glance

Table of Contents

Introduction

Once upon time, just a few years ago, seminars and meetings occurred in conference rooms and auditoriums. If you couldn't figure out how to get there or crib some notes from your friend or colleague, you missed out.

Then along came the webinar. It changed everything, that is, as soon as you understood what it actually did. Now if you were thinking *webinar* is a word that hasn't been around for long, you'd be correct. Why is that?

Webinar belongs to a class of words known as a *portmanteau*. It's when a new word is formed from two others to best reflect a contemporary practice or concept. We've been doing it for ages, although we seem to forget. For example, when we needed a word for that mealtime between breakfast and lunch, it became known as *brunch*. *Televangelist* logically refers to a television evangelist, just as *jorts* are jeans and shorts. Then there's the colloquial ones like *bromance*, *chillax*, and *staycation*, which respectively refer to the platonic relationship between two male buddies, chilling out and relaxing, and of course, the stay-at-home vacation.

That brings us back to *webinar*, which derives its name from web and seminar to describe a meeting that takes place over the Internet. The term *meeting* can mean a lot of different things, but in the scenario of the webinar, it simply refers to the means of using the Internet to create a space that's accessible via nearby computer screen or web-enabled mobile device, as opposed to a banquet hall or conference room.

This virtual meeting pays no heed to geographical boundaries or times zones and behaves much like interactive television on a global scale. That means the meeting held at noon in New York can accommodate participants in Seattle, London, Tokyo, and just about anyplace else that has an Internet connection. Beside the issue of someone getting up early or staying up late, the meeting takes place in real time with full interactivity.

Many times the webinar shares a similar structure to a conference call, but with the added luxury of visual communication, and often better production values. A decade or so ago, if someone said they could reap the benefits of a physical meeting while sitting in front of a screen, it would have harkened back to an episode of the futuristic cartoon *The Jetsons*.

Maybe you would have thought of a webinar as the basis for one of those "what technology could be" commercials. If someone told you that you could watch over your computer, you might have been a little amazed. But if someone told you that you could watch on your cell phone, you would have thought they were crazy. It wasn't something that would happen any time soon.

Jet ahead to 2014. Every day, more and more people from all walks of society are participating in some form of a webinar. Just about any gathering that used to be held in a physical venue works now as a webinar.

Just because you have the technology at your disposal doesn't mean you can pull off a great webinar without doing the necessary work. Just like the meeting in the physical world, if you don't plan it right, you will give your audience more of an opportunity to check their eyelids for holes than interpret your message. Worse, in a physical meeting, your attendees are unlikely to walk out if they get bored, but in a webinar, it's easy for them to log off.

Conversely, if you do it right, they will stay for the whole session, and not only return for your next one, but also tell their friends and colleagues about the experience. The intention of this book is to give you the tools to make the latter happen.

About This Book

I'm not a fan of overly procedural technical books, opting instead for the get-in and get-out style of reference manuals. *Webinars For Dummies* helps make sense of this cool communication technology in a fun way. And hopefully, you'll find that it goes much further than those boring manuals that seem to camouflage information in a sea of words. Those are not much different than doing a word search amongst a giant page of letters in one of those pads printed on pulpy paper. No pulpy paper here: Instead, the vital information is up-close and right to the point.

As a result, this book covers the nuts and bolts producing a webinar, while at the same time addressing the outside influences that make it work too. For example, using social media has little to do with actually running the webinar, but it certainly helps let people know that it exists. The same holds for understanding how to write an effective invitation, using sensible aesthetics with PowerPoint, and properly using video.

It's also important to provide tips and techniques that help the presenter entertain and inform the audience. All of these will help you produce a more balanced webinar. Like so many things in life, the art of success has to do with how well you integrate areas that aren't always related to actual webinar production, yet are still essential.

Crucial information includes an overview of the webinar, the effectiveness of different formats, and how to produce top-notch content to support the discussion. Although these are heavily addressed in this book, I also talk about some cool techniques and advice to help dazzle your audience. That's because webinars do not need to be stuffy and boring. Instead, you can entertain your audience as you inform them.

Although the content of this book is brief and to the point, it's less about being the fast-food equivalent of information and more like a smorgasbord of resources. Here are a few tips to help you navigate this book and its content.

New terms are *italicized*. Website addresses appear in a special font, like `www.dummies.com/`. Sidebars present information that is interesting, but not absolutely essential.

Foolish Assumptions

Whether you've successfully produced a webinar in the past, or just learned the meaning of the word, there's something in this book for you. That's because its approach deals both with the intricacies of webinar production and the non-production topics that relate to it. Topics such as writing an effective invitation and using social media to support the webinar go beyond the mechanics of putting a webinar together, yet they're all equally important. So although each reader comes to the table from a different place, you can dine on exactly what you need.

Newbies

If you're a newbie, *webinar* is a word that has recently entered your vocabulary and you like its potential for getting your message out to the masses. Now you want to produce one for your next event, but you're not really sure what it takes to do it. Well, you came to the right place. This book picks up the topic for you right after the merger of the words *World Wide Web* and *seminar*, taking you on a journey comparable to going from sandlot baseball to the Major Leagues.

Business managers

Most likely, you're already familiar with the power of a webinar, but not fully knowledgeable about the various aspects of putting one together. You may already know how to produce a webinar, or at least how the good ones are structured. What you may not know are the best practices to promote it, or how to take advantage of social media. Well, you came to the right place. Regardless of your experience level, you will succinctly find answers to your lingering questions and get back to what you do best.

Presenters

Regardless whether you know your way around a webinar or want to start learning about them pronto, this book will help fill in the gaps for you. You may find the chapters and sections that deal with the roles in the webinar helpful, as well the sections that provide advice for moderators, presenters, and producers.

Producers

Perhaps you're looking to expand the scope of your next webinar with high-definition video, or want to try moderating a multi-speaker panel. The good news is that you can find information on these topics and a few other advanced ones in this book. In addition to familiarizing you with these practices, this book provides quick reference info for you when you're explaining things to less-experienced members of your team.

How This Book Is Organized

Webinars For Dummies is divided into five parts. Each details the various phases of producing your webinar as effectively as possible. Because the book covers a wide swath of topics and information, each reader will no doubt have a preference when it comes to a particular area. Some may relish the section that pertains to getting started and others may skip ahead to the chapters detailing topics beyond the webinar. Still others will bolster their understanding of effectively using social media, the best technique for multi-camera video, or how to create effective PowerPoint slides. It doesn't matter where you start — it's all here for you. Think of it as a variety pack of information where everyone gets exactly what they need.

Part I: Getting Started with Webinars

Part I provides the reader with a basic understanding of the webinar and how it's made the world smaller when it comes to holding a conference. This section offers an overview of the webinar, making initial plans, and putting together an effective team.

Part II: Preparing an Effective Webinar

Covering all the pieces that make up the webinar, this collection of chapters addresses the preparation and planning that go into making an effective webinar, from finding the right platform and planning and creating material, to the most effective methods for reaching out to potential participants.

Part III: The Day of the Show

Part III focuses on the big day, covering aspects like maximizing the role of the presenter, engaging the audience, and making sure all is right for the video portion of the show.

Part IV: Beyond the Webinar

If the first three parts deal with everything necessary to build a webinar from the ground up, Part IV deals with the day after, when you're trying to figure out how to follow up what you've done and extend the life of your content. This collection of chapters explains how to get the most value out of your event and to capitalize on this tool.

Part V: The Part of Tens

The traditional closer for all *For Dummies* books offers top-ten lists. This one includes two lists: ten tips for successful webinars and ten common webinar mistakes and how to avoid them. Each provides quick answers to common questions and concerns.

Icons Used in This Book

What's a . . . *For Dummies* book without icons pointing you in the direction of really great information that's sure to help you along your way? In this section, I briefly describe each icon used in this book.

This icon marks a generally interesting and useful fact — something you might want to remember for later.

This icon points out helpful suggestions and useful nuggets of information.

When you see this icon, you know that there's techie stuff nearby. If you're not feeling very techie, feel free to skip it.

The Warning icon highlights lurking danger. With this icon, I'm telling you to pay attention and proceed with caution.

Beyond the Book

- **Cheat Sheet:** This book's Cheat Sheet can be found online at `www.dummies.com/cheatsheet/webinars`. See the Cheat Sheet for tips on how to plan your webinar and pointers on driving higher registration.
- **Dummies.com online articles:** Companion articles to this book's content can be found online at `www.dummies.com/extras/webinars`. The topics range from figuring out how to make the end of the webinar the beginning of the conversation with your customer to tips on using video effectively.
- **Updates:** If this book has any updates after printing, they will be posted to `www.dummies.com/extras/webinars`.

Where to Go from Here

Democracy rules with this book, and while everyone from the novice to the experienced can get something from its hallowed pages, not everybody needs to read cover to cover unless you really want to make my day. With a book written in this style, there are several inalienable facts. Some readers will find a portion of the information too basic, whereas others will deem some topics too advanced. Others are somewhere in the middle. You know who you are, so feel free to flip, skim, and even jump past anything that doesn't pertain to your interests or understanding on any given day. You can always come back to it tomorrow.

Regardless of your familiarity with webinar production, you will still probably want to look at the Tip, Warning, and Remember icons. Then there's the lists — there's no shortage of them if you're looking for quick information. Take a gander and soak up what you need to know.

Part I

Getting Started with Webinars

Visit www.dummies.com for more great content online.

In this part . . .

- Understand how to build Excel tables that hold and store the data you need to analyze.
- Find quick and easy ways to begin your analysis using simple statistics, sorting, and filtering.
- Get practical stratagems and commonsense tactics for grabbing data from extra sources.
- Discover tools for cleaning and organizing the raw data you want to analyze.

Chapter 1

Webinars with Maximum Impact

In This Chapter

- Describing the webinar
- Understanding the tools of the webinar
- Grasping the roles of producing a webinar
- Understanding what a webinar can do for you

In the 1960s animated sitcom *The Jetsons*, George Jetson did a lot of business via a television screen from his office at Spacely's Space Sprockets. The futuristic show imagined the future of the workplace and beyond, and that particular scenario came true with the webinar.

Nowadays, thanks to webinars, people can channel their inner George Jetson and attend meetings from anyplace they choose.

Getting a Handle on Webinars

Webinars are a newer kind of meeting with a funny name that allow you to attend from home or office — anywhere with Internet access, actually.

Who doesn't like that kind of meeting? If you were ask anyone to describe their favorite kind of meeting, besides them saying none at all, they'll usually choose ones that are most comfortable. How often are those industrial-type office chairs comfortable, especially when you're sitting in them for more than an hour? *Almost never* is a likely guess, unless you compare it to sitting on its non-cushioned folding chair cousin. Then it's a clear never!

But when you allow your audience to trade in some utilitarian area for the comfort of their home, office, or on the road, you have them relaxed and attentive when listening to your message.

That's why webinars are so fantastic. They let you hold a meeting from a remote location that participants can join from their own computer. Not only are the participants comfortable and less stressed (commuting and travel do take their toll, after all), but you can also throw in some cool technology like video and PowerPoint presentations.

Yes, the webinar has changed the meeting game.

Much like the telephone, shown in Figure 1-1, made the location of a conversation between two people irrelevant, the webinar has done the same for the traditional meeting or seminar. Combine that idea with video and information graphics, and beam it out to thousands of people, and you see the value of the webinar.

Figure 1-1: The rotary dial telephone enabled communication between people in different locations.

What a webinar is

Although webinars are a relatively new concept, many people have at least heard of them. Whether they can accurately describe one is another story. No worries. If you can't, let me take a stab at it. Basically, a *webinar* is a communication between two or more individuals over the Internet that uses audio, video, and interactive technology. Unlike a group chat in a glassed conference room, a book club discussion in your living room, or a large gathering in a public lecture hall, the meeting takes place wherever the participants are located.

So although the host resides in one location, the attendees can participate from anywhere there's an Internet connection. In some ways, a webinar is like a telephone conference call on steroids, but at the same time, it's very different.

Comparing a webinar to a conference call shares the same logic as thinking a 1928 Model A, as seen in Figure 1-2, does the same thing as a 2013 Cadillac Escalade. Sure, both will get you to your destination, but one clearly offers more comfort, efficiency, and style. Unless you're an antique car aficionado, the Escalade appears the more logical choice. And so is the webinar.

Figure 1-2: This 1928 Ford Model A doesn't offer the same amenities as a luxury vehicle.

One reason a webinar is better than a telephone conference is its ability to go beyond audio communication by bringing an interactive visual component to the meeting. Sometimes that component is as simple as a few title slides or pie charts, but sometimes, it's a full-blown PowerPoint presentation with video. Add live chat and microphones on the user end, and you've created a situation where participants can communicate with each other as well as with the moderator.

More elaborate productions have a moderated panel like your own version of *The McLaughlin Group*, replete with multiple camera setups. (If you're not sure what *The McLaughlin Group* is, just think about those Sunday morning news shows with a bunch of talking heads sitting around arguing.)

Here's the basics of how webinars work:

- **Similar in some ways to a physical meeting:** Both physical meetings and webinars bring large groups together for a discussion of topics, but with the webinar, the attendees aren't all in the same room and can be located anywhere.
- **Each has its own structure:** Like any type of meeting, webinars vary greatly, yet they also share a common thread with a physical meeting space. Both use a moderator who explains the agenda, sets up the

PowerPoint presentation, and shares other appropriate content with the audience. Of course, with a webinar, it doesn't matter where the audience is located.

- **Uses audio and visual aids:** Audio and video are shared over the Internet through a webinar tool. Audio usually broadcasts through each participant's computer or over a telephone line. To participate, you need a computer with speakers and an Internet connection.

What a webinar isn't

REMEMBER

Now that you know what a webinar is, I want to examine what it's not, compared to similar technology. For example, many people think that it's the same thing as a streamed event. A streamed event shares more in common with a television broadcast, like the one seen in Figure 1-3, than a webinar. In the physical world, you would never confuse attending a PTA meeting at your kid's school with going to a comedy club, nor would you think that going to movies is the same as attending a condominium board meeting. That's because some of these examples provide interaction, and some of them don't.

Figure 1-3: A circa 1950s television set.

Here's some food for thought on everything that a webinar is *not:*

- **A television broadcast:** A webinar is not an infomercial. Thank goodness, because who wants to hear a customer comment on how succulent the chicken is when cooked in some miracle apparatus advertised on late-night TV?
- **One-way presentation:** You know the type — where the audience can only watch and listen like a live streamed event.
- **An all-day affair:** You wouldn't want to sit through an eight-hour meeting in your workplace or some banquet hall, so why would you want to stare that long at a computer screen? The best webinars are carefully scheduled and have a managed running time that allows for bathroom breaks. People tend to lose interest when anything runs too long.

Why Do Webinars Work?

It's a win-win arrangement for both the presenter and participants. Everybody gets something out of it, with the participants being pretty darn comfortable in the process. That's because webinars offer a pleasing blend of technology and convenience.

Besides reaching a broad audience, the webinar can allow each participant to have a voice in the meeting or session. That kind of participation rarely works in a conference room, and almost never does in a large space. For example, some people are shy when it comes to speaking in conference room, just as others hog the floor with questions and comments. And when the meeting is in a larger space like a banquet hall, few people, with the exception of those seated in the front, get picked to ask a question, so most people get lost in the crowd.

Webinars also make life easier for the producer. Instead of having the added responsibility of securing an appropriately sized venue and all the things that go with it, you can concentrate on getting your message together and allow the service provider to worry about the rest.

Here are some others reasons that webinars work, including

- **They're affordable.** Travel costs, car rentals, and meals are greatly reduced or non-existent.
- **Location is irrelevant.** Participants can log on from just about anywhere. Of course, if you're with a Sherpa heading up Everest, perhaps this doesn't apply to you.

- **They're time zone-proof.** Anyone who wants to can join, although for some, it's morning, others afternoon, and for those on the eastern fringe, tomorrow, as seen in the quartet of clocks in Figure 1-4.
- **They provide flexibility.** An impromptu meeting takes time to come together because you have to consider location and people's schedules. But with a webinar, companies can schedule meetings or training sessions on short notice without worrying about the location of the participants.

Figure 1-4: Participants can join in a webinar no matter the time.

And participants reap the benefits too:

- **Webinars are interactive.** They provide real-time interaction between participants and presenter.
- **Participants can watch on-demand.** Participants can watch an archived version of the webinar if they missed it, or if they simply want to watch it again.
- **They're cost-effective.** You can save money on travel, food, and other stuff that the company doesn't cover.

Save on expenses

The best things in life are free, but webinars usually are not one of them. The costs to facilitate a webinar can range from free to expensive, but even "free" ones have some operating costs involved. Some providers charge a monthly flat fee, but it's a good idea to do some research and find the provider and plan that are best for your needs and budget.

Still, using a powerful communication tool to reach out to people saves more than gasoline or jet fuel.

These direct and indirect savings include

REMEMBER

- **Increased productivity:** When your employees don't need to travel, they have more time to be productive. For example, they don't have to stop working on a project because they need to get to the airport or drive a couple of hours.
- **Lower venue costs:** This means you won't need to worry about finding a large room or venue and those overhead costs normally associated with having a meeting on location.
- **Decreased budget for support services:** These include chairs, refreshments, and so on.

Provide two-way communication

TIP

When you're watching the president on television delivering the State of the Union address, you're among an audience of approximately 35 million getting a progress report on the nation. Putting your political feelings aside — and the annoyance of having your favorite show pre-empted — it's an effective way of letting the country know what's going on.

That same model has limited appeal, however, when it comes to issues and topics that *directly* affect the individual. For example, employees don't want to hear their company president deliver a speech on changes to work procedures over the next calendar year. That type of meeting compels people to *interact* in some way. Why? Because people being able to ask questions at a meeting is a key part of the process.

REMEMBER

Two-way communication lets the presenter and the participant exchange information by providing the chance to ask questions or participate. Although participants can't just blurt out questions, they at least have the chance to participate using a variety of methods. By letting everyone participate despite their location, webinars lead to a more effective meeting experience.

Here are a few means for communicating that go beyond what you as a participant see onscreen:

- **Telephone:** Many webinars rely on using a telephone for audio purposes, so you can hear the presenter and ask live questions. Be ready to ask a question or add input when you're called upon and be sure to identify yourself. After all, nobody knows who you are on the other side of the screen.
- **Headset:** Connecting a headset to your computer allows you to listen and speak at the webinar. Just remember to mute your microphone when you're not speaking.

- **Social media:** Some webinars allow participants to ask questions and make comments using Facebook or Twitter. The comments or questions either run on a ticker or are answered by the moderator.
- **E-mail:** Participants can send questions in advance, and the moderator will read them aloud, time permitting, and answer them.
- **Text message:** Just like e-mail questions, the moderator can read and answer these questions. Comments can also run on a ticker on the bottom of the screen during the presentation.

Ideal for global mobile audiences

As more companies realize the value of employees not having to schlep into the office, at least part of the time, the webinar becomes one more great thing about telecommuting. Webinars provide the perfect confluence of being able to work your normal job from home, while at the same time providing the ability to attend a meeting that, not that long ago, you'd have to commute to.

Webinars allow the participant to take an active role in the meeting, doing everything from listening to the meeting to being a contributor (responding to polls, asking questions, chatting), all from the comfort of home office.

Here some other benefits:

- **Relaxed environment:** There's no place like home. When you're comfortable and relaxed, you can more effectively absorb the material coming at you and interact accordingly.
- **Cost effective:** For so many reasons, webinars benefit the commuter, including not having to battle traffic jams, burn excessive gas, or put miles on your car. In addition, your blood pressure will thank you.
- **No worry of what to wear:** Heck, since you're at home, you can wear whatever you want and no one is the wiser. The value of this cannot be underestimated, no matter how many times it's repeated.
- **Increased productivity:** By alleviating the stress of commuting, you can use that energy to participate and absorb the full scope of the webinar.

Can be live or later

REMEMBER

Face it. Life happens, and sometimes people miss important events. But with webinars, you don't need to rely on a colleague to find out what happened. Anybody who has ever played Telephone knows that information a step or two removed from its source gets lost in translation. Webinars are different.

Say you missed the webinar. Instead of asking a friend, coworker, or fellow participant what happened, you can simply watch it later. You see, webinars are often recorded, thus allowing viewers to watch them on demand from the host's website. Think of it as broadcasting over the Internet. Even if you've seen it before, watching the archived version again allows you to stop, pause, and rewind at your own pace.

TIP

Just be aware that it's a very large file if you plan on downloading. Some sites will store it online for a limited time. Check with your webinar provider to find out how long it will be available.

Here are a few other things to consider:

- **Recording is optional.** Some services include recording the webinar, whereas others offer it as an option. Free webinar sites generally do not include this service.
- **You can do it yourself.** Screen capture programs like Snapz Pro (`www.ambrosiasw.com`) or Debut Video Capture (`www.nchsoftware.com`), as seen in Figure 1-5, allow you to capture whatever is on your screen and play it back as a movie.
- **You can share the link with others.** When the archived version is available, send out an e-mail blast with meeting highlights and a link to the recorded version. This provides an opportunity for people who missed the meeting to watch it, as well as those who did watch it to view it again.

Figure 1-5: Record a webinar with Debut Video Capture.

Understanding the Tools of a Webinar

A physical meeting — you know, one that's held in a conference room or the back of a local pub — still requires more than a group of people to make it happen. Otherwise, that scenario may involve someone continuously repeating, "Can you hear me now?" If you don't want to stand up and scream at the others so they can all hear, you need some basic equipment.

Sometimes all you need are chairs, a podium for the speaker, and a microphone to transform a room full of people into a meeting. Other times, it takes a little more. The same holds true for the webinar. It requires some electronic and technical gear to make it work.

Although each webinar varies, all of them need the proper conferencing tools, including computers, software, and an Internet connection to broadcast. On the receiving end, the participant needs the proper coordinates to access the webinar and a web-enabled device. That covers a lot of ground, and I touch on the details later in the book. The recipe for a successful webinar has much in common with preparing a fine meal: Both depend on the finest ingredients.

Computer

Many newer computers, like the Apple MacBook Air shown in Figure 1-6, can handle the minimum requirements of a webinar. Both newer Windows and Macintosh machines work fine. When it comes to older units and operating systems, check with your webinar platform provider to determine the proper minimum requirements for your webinar.

Software

REMEMBER

For the most part, the application that runs your webinar is associated with a provider and level of service. Also known as a *webinar tool*, the software is the heart and soul of the operation. Take the time to find the one that works best for your needs. Many services offer a variety of choices to match your needs and budget. There's a learning curve and eventual comfort factor with any software that plays a role too. Select a service that matches your needs and budget. Be sure that the chosen provider provides support and basic training.

Consider the following when weighing your options:

- **Why do you need a webinar?** What do you plan do with your webinar? Is it for training purposes, work-related meetings, or for marketing a new product?

Figure 1-6: An Apple MacBook Air.

- **Who are your participants?** Is this for a general audience, or will the topic be specialized? Also, will your organization incur all of the costs, or will they charge participants to attend?
- **How many people do you want to reach?** Depending on the plan and type of service, you can reach anywhere from a few to a few thousand participants. Free services or a low-priced option offer limited features, including limits on the number of people at your webinar, whereas high-end packages support tens of thousands of participants at each session.
- **What is your budget?** If you frequently wish to connect with only 10–12 people and don't care about recording your webinar for later viewing, some of the free plans might work for you. More elaborate plans range in price from a few dollars to thousands per month. Do you want a flat-fee service that provides everything, or do you just want to pay for what you need? Usually that means paying per participant, with time, audio services, recording, and toll-free phone being paid for à la carte.

Video

If a picture is worth a thousand words, what happens when you multiply that figure by 29.97 frames per second? Wow, it sounds like a few seconds of video can add up to a lot of words. But more importantly, the audience sees the speaker talking and observes body language, so nothing gets lost in translation. In addition, you can illustrate certain topics with compelling video footage.

Here are a few ways webinars use video:

- **Single camera setup:** Usually the single camera is trained on the moderator. Sometimes it's a static shot, meaning that the camera position doesn't change. Other times, an operator changes the camera angle or zooms in and out.
- **Multi-camera:** More sophisticated techniques use more than a single camera. Because a webinar is live, this setup requires a technical director. (See the "Technical director" section later in the chapter for more details.) A multi-camera setup would be used for shooting a moderated panel to show the entire group and for capturing individuals as they speak or react to another speaker.
- **Webcam:** Cheap, affordable, and common, the built-in camera that comes with most new computers and web-enabled devices allows users to make their presence known. As seen in Figure 1-7, webcam video is great for a bare-bones webinar, or one where the participants want, or need, to see each other on screen.
- **File video:** You may want to show video content to illustrate a topic. Footage can either reside on your computer or be found online at sites such as YouTube or Vimeo.

Figure 1-7: Webcam video is not always flattering, but it's easy to use, included on most computers, and is better than no video at all.

High-speed Internet

In the world of the webinar, the need for a fast online connection seems as obvious as needing air to breathe or food to survive. That's because the high-speed pipeline is the essential bloodline for your webinar, allowing video and presentation to play smoothly and not skip or randomly stop. Broadcasting these materials requires a significant amount of bandwidth. That means the pipe has to let a lot of information pass through it seamlessly. Cable, DSL, and satellite providers are offering faster modems, as seen in Figure 1-8, to meet your need for speed.

But *high-speed* is a relative term. Some connections are clearly faster than others. That's why you need to consider the slower side of connection. That means you should be conscious of image size, video quality, and the tempo of the show.

Figure 1-8: A cable modem.

Going mobile with some cool devices

Those pee-wee sized mobile devices that allow you to read books and check e-mail can also connect you to the latest webinar. Thanks to their alphanumeric touch screens or mini keyboards, you can fully participate while you're on the go. You can even wirelessly connect a keyboard to give you greater control over what you need to say.

These devices include

- **Smartphone:** Whether it's your Apple iPhone, Blackberry, Android, or some other phone, you can watch and participate in a webinar on your mobile phone.
- **Tablet:** An all-in-one computing device that includes a camera, microphone, touchscreen, built-in Wi-Fi, and sometimes even 4G connectivity. (Or you can just say it looks like a giant smartphone that doesn't make phone calls.) The Apple iPad, Samsung Galaxy, and the Google Nexus are a few models. This extends to the iPod Touch, which also has Wi-Fi capability.
- **Laptop:** Use your laptop computer anywhere there's a Wi-Fi signal, and when there's not, you can even use a cellular card or MiFi from wherever there's signal strength to make a phone call.

Getting to Know the People in Your Webinar

Say you've signed up with one of those free webinar sites to hold a meeting for ten or twelve people, knowing there's a good chance you'll do everything from moderating the discussion to taking questions afterward. Maybe you like wearing different hats from producer to presenter. Although that sort of multitasking is fine on a smaller level, it's not practical as you begin to reach out to a larger audience. Sophisticated webinars simply require a bigger team.

How big? The size of your webinar depends on your needs, budget, and intended reach, so that dictates the size of your team. In the next few sections, I take a look at every role in producing a webinar, with the idea that most of the time, not every head wears a single hat.

Presenter

REMEMBER

Also described as moderator and host, the *presenter* provides a face — and sometimes more appropriately, a voice — to the webinar. Think of this role as a combination of talk-show host Jimmy Fallon, a preacher, and your college chemistry professor. That means the entertainment-to-information ratio varies, depending on both the topic and the presenter.

Sometimes the person in this role clearly sounds like an expert and acts as the main source of information. Other times, the host introduces topics and various speakers. Besides acting as the master of ceremonies, the presenter also creates annotations, highlights important areas, and creates markings on the screen to help get the point across to the audience. The ability to entertain while at the same time leading, inspiring, and motivating the audience is a pretty positive quality for this role. Regardless of what you call it, the art of this job is getting through the program with flawless precision. Some large-scale webinars include several presenters, usually with one taking the role as the main presenter.

Producer

A *producer* is the person who takes all the different pieces and makes them work together. Sometimes it's the same person who is presenting the show. Other times, the producer is the head of a large team. Basically, the producer has a hand in everything from planning the webinar to making sure all of its aspects run smoothly. That includes managing the production from inception all the way to presenting it to an audience.

Director

Sometimes the balance between humans and technology requires some prodding. Actually, just getting humans to do something requires prodding too. If the webinar were a television show, the *director* would make sure that everyone was in place during the entire shoot. They do the same for your webinar, at least in some capacity. Having a director is essential for large-scale productions, especially with a merger of segments, technology, and people. Remember, if there's a glitch, the audience isn't always patient enough to stick around.

Writer

One of the things that separate a webinar from a video blog is its structure, and much of that comes from working with a good script created by a skilled *writer*. Good writing is also the secret to energizing the audience as you carefully weave the prime topics into the program while providing a touch of theatricality. It all begins with a good script.

Stage manager

A *stage manager* controls what happens on the set, or near it, making sure that everything in the right place and that everything goes as planned. That goes beyond telling people to turn off their cell phones. For large-scale productions, the role of the stage manager relies on making sure that everyone and everything is in the right place, which is essential when it comes to a moderated panel.

Technical director

The technical director (TD) makes sure that all of the technical aspects go off without a hitch. More than likely, the technical director deals with video, especially on those multiple camera setups used for large-scale events like a webinar that uses the interview format, or perhaps a moderated panel. Someone has to manage the different camera feeds, so the TD communicates with each camera operator and switches the appropriate angle out to viewers. Because a webinar is live, there's no time to edit, so the technical director edits on the fly by switching to the appropriate camera angle. This role differs from other webinars that include less video, where the technical director also makes sure the audio and video components are working properly. Responsibilities include making sure the webinar connection stays up, as well as monitoring audio and transmission-related stuff.

Audience supervisor

For really big webinars that have a live audience, it's important to have someone focusing on the audience perspective, both on and off site. The audience supervisor monitors the audience and communicates their issues and concerns regarding the webinar. In addition, they may field questions for the Q&A period. Monitors who scour social media during the webinar looking for important information sometimes support this position.

You wearing all the hats

When it comes to very large webinars, it's entirely possible that a team of experts fills all of these roles individually, depending on the size, format, and intended reach of the audience. But most presentations require only a few people for a modest presentation, and depending on your confidence, it's entirely possible to do it all on your own. So if you're bona fide do-it-yourselfer, technology has evolved to the point where a single business user can quickly and easily produce a pretty spectacular webinar at the comfort of your own desk.

Gauging Effective Uses for a Webinar

Webinars have created a true David and Goliath moment, with the size of an organization not playing a factor in its reach and scope. The small upstart that covers three counties in northern California can technically reach the same audience of a multinational corporation.

Although it's a level playing field, you still need to let people know about the topic of your webcast. Entire books are dedicated to techniques for reaching out to a mass audience, but you can start with an e-mail blast and by using social media like Facebook and Twitter.

Webinars also share some similarities to a physical meeting in that both provide a forum for reaching out to large groups of people. Both are live performances that make the audience an important part of the process. And like their physical counterpart, webinars come in many sizes and styles. Yet, the webinar offers some clear advantages that go beyond making the participant feel like they're in an episode of *The Jetsons*.

Employee meetings

Distance no longer acts as a nemesis to those not near the meeting site. Whether they're across the country or around the globe, webinars can bring employees together. Topics range from changes in their 401(k), preparation for an upcoming sales conference, or those quarterly staff meetings — you know, the ones that happen just for the heck of it. Even if the webinar is about the new water cooler, these meetings keep everyone informed, and more importantly let them get back to work immediately.

Why it's effective:

- Lets employees get back to work right away
- Saves on travel
- Convenience promotes attention

Training sessions

What if you logged onto to a webinar that explained how to produce a webinar? (Would it be like looking in the mirror?) Now imagine you can use this format to teach and train people on a whole variety of things. Whether you're an educational provider, a family historian, or company that needs to bring staff up-to-date on new technology, webinars can reach a wide audience.

Why it's effective:

- Keeps staff up to date on procedure
- Incurs fewer lost work hours
- Brings the classroom to the comfortable environment of the computer screen

Marketing

Technology and marketing have always had a productive marriage and that relationship has gotten a second honeymoon with the webinar. That's because companies have always depended on meetings and demonstrations to generate new business. But meetings did have a high cost, especially travel and venue expenses. Taking location out of the equation makes them affordable and saves time.

Why it's effective:

- Gets the word out quicker
- Is convenient for both the marketer and potential customer
- Lets you bring the presentation to multiple locations simultaneously

Talent development

Talent development includes training new hires and developing employees for leadership positions within your organization. In addition, today more than ever, organizations are changing procedures and adapting new policies, so it's important for staff to be aware of it. In a sense, it's like organizational education, and that's become essential for both organizations and the individual because it provides a breeding ground for future managers and specialists.

Webinars make this process more accessible by allowing the interested parties to determine when and where to participate in any work-related sessions. Sometimes that takes place while they're sitting at their desk in front of their computer screen. Other times, it's on the treadmill at the gym from their smartphone.

Why it's effective:

- Enables efficient training of personnel and saves time
- Provides both the organization and individual with opportunity
- Effectively communicates to organizations and individuals

Chapter 2

Planning Your Webinar

In This Chapter

- Establishing the goal of your webinar
- Picking the format that works for you
- Selecting the talent
- Structuring the webinar

Life has few certainties, with the short list including death and taxes. Those have ridden the top of the charts longer than "Stairway to Heaven" and "Layla" have made the perennial list of greatest rock songs. But down a little bit from those oldies but goodies on the non-musical compilation is another prophetic certainty: *Poor planning leads to poor production*. Now in all fairness, sometimes even well-planned events fail for one reason or another. Yet, rarely, if ever, does poor planning lead to an impressive presentation. Can you imagine deciding to get married on a Wednesday, and having an elegant reception for 200 people that coming Saturday? Or winging it when you take your bar exam for the first time and passing with flying colors? So rather than taking any chances with your next — or first-ever — webinar, in this chapter, I show you the basics required for putting it together from the ground up.

Setting a Goal for Your Webinar

What's your webinar trying to say? Is it something like, "I have something that's going to change your life." Or maybe it's "I bet you didn't know this." These sound inviting enough to take a chance and register for the webinar.

Other times, however, webinar topics have a less appealing voice that, when translated, sounds like "(Yawn) I'm boring," or "Here's a bland idea." Or maybe, "It will take up an hour of your life that you're never getting back." Don't let that be you.

Whether you're attempting to inform employees of upcoming changes in their health insurance coverage, mounting a marketing campaign for a new kind of business intelligence solution, or conducting a training session on a state-of-the-art jackhammer with a built-in MP3 player that removes your wrinkles while you use it, consider the webinar successful if it informs the audience, no matter how sensible, important, or ridiculous the topic. As long as you can deliver what was promised, hold their attention doing it, and entertain them along the way, the potential is boundless.

Webinars succeed and fail for many reasons, with the root cause of either being your ability to clearly define the goal.

This is easier said than done, apparently, because some webinars are just plain boring. Names like "Third Quarter Statistics" and "Analyzing Web-Based Analytics" sound like a snooze-fest to a potential participant. Not many folks are enticed to online meetings that use words such as *analyze*, *extrapolate*, or even *aggregate* in their titles, no matter how exciting the content promised. Make sure your webinar has an interesting title.

Then there are webinars that never meet their objective before running out of time. Those are like the webinar equivalent of that co-worker or neighbor who rambles on and on without getting to the point. It's not that we don't want to give them the time of day, but their method of communication makes us look at our watch as if we were late for something (which is embarrassing because few of us wear a watch anymore).

It's not much different when it comes to webinars. In fact, they introduce another wrinkle, especially when you realize you cannot see your audience. And yes, that matters. So much of what we do comes from the immediate feedback we get from human contact. Make a comment to the person next to you during your overseas flight, and chances are, if they smile, you proceed to make small talk. If they look away or give you a deadpan nod, you know conversation is not going to happen.

The webinar doesn't provide the luxury of allowing you to see your audience, so you need to have a clear goal and structure it so that it covers all that you've promised, but not so much that it overloads the audience. It's hard to overstress the importance of having a goal. Just as two friends may develop a loose itinerary for their upcoming road trip, your meeting should always have a purpose, no matter how simple.

When the point of a conversation isn't entirely obvious, the listener becomes disinterested. So be clear, concise, and goal-oriented, like in Figure 2-1.

Figure 2-1: A soccer ball hits the net for a goal.

Picking Your Poison . . . er, Format

After you've clarified what you're trying to convey to your audience, it's important to figure out the best way to deliver that message. Depending on the topic and the voices that you wish to include, it should be simple to pick the proper format. Sometimes the format is obvious. For example, if it's a CEO introducing a new product, the format should be something in the flavor of what Steve Jobs did whenever Apple introduced a new technology. That's the single-speaker approach. Launching something like the iPhone with a moderated panel of guest speakers would not work.

In the next few sections, I make a few suggestions for getting your message across.

Single speaker

REMEMBER

Think of a single-speaker event as similar to a speech or lecture, where a single individual hosts the event, follows the program, sets up graphics and presentations, and moderates the question-and-answer period. This presentation should rarely run longer than one hour, and sometimes that's pushing it. Why? Because people get tired of looking at the same talking head or listening to the same voice, no matter how enthusiastic, after a while!

Situations that work for this kind of webinar include

- Lectures
- Product introductions
- Implementation of new policies
- Speeches

Interview style

It's not *60 Minutes* exactly, nor should you try to imitate it. Still, this format consists of a host interviewing one or more people during the webinar. The interview format provides a different perspective and compels the audience with multiple layers of information by including alternate voices and opinions.

Variations include

- **Experts:** It's always refreshing to the audience when the moderator interviews a subject matter expert on a particular topic.
- **Different perspective:** This lets the audience see a slightly different side of the topic.
- **Testimonials:** These are first-hand accounts by someone affected by the topic.

Moderated panel

If you've ever watched *Real Time with Bill Maher* or *The McLaughlin Group*, you can see how unruly things can get when the format includes several speakers with differing opinions. A *moderated panel* is a more elaborate format that provides your audience with a controlled discussion by a panel of speakers. The secret to its success demands a lot from the host, who must maintain the flow by wearing the hats of leader, entertainer, and referee. Sometimes things get unruly and the moderator must keep the speakers from talking over each other and getting into the occasional fistfight. (Okay, the last one probably won't happen.)

Although the moderated panel offers the potential of being the most informative, entertaining, and compelling format to present your webinar, it's also the type that requires the most planning to make it work. Obviously, when more pieces are involved, it makes getting them all in synch all the more important, but it's hard to rehearse a moderated panel because the panelists make it challenging to gauge the flow.

Here are a few situations where this type of meeting works best:

TIP

- **When there are a few topics to discuss:** The host usually introduces herself and the panel to the webinar audience, sets up the topics for discussion, and carefully makes sure the topics do not run over their allotted time period.
- **When a well-balanced approach is essential:** This works with situations that do not have a clear answer, so the multiple voices provide additional perspective for the audience.
- **For a question-and-answer session:** By allowing participants to ask questions, you can provide the web audience with a wide ranges of thoughts and opinions on the subject.

Real-time audience data

Audience feedback collection has come a long way over the years when simple graphics included information that was up to date, that is, if you considered the week or so before the event and it went to the printer up to date. Since the pie chart was invented, sometime after the pie, the circle with the internal triangles has been a staple in meetings to define the progress of various performance-related issues.

The pie chart is still a part of the webinar meeting, but because webinars take place on the Internet in 2014 and not in a conference room in 1964, it's been updated to deliver up-to-the-moment statistics, as opposed to stale information from some old survey. In fact, you can poll your audience during the webinar and present *those* facts after compiling them in a pie chart.

REMEMBER

Of course, pie charts are only one way to present information in graphic form. But if you choose to use a pie chart, consider it a fresh alternative with modern technology at your disposal. Feel free to use it to accomplish these and other tasks:

TIP

- **Poll:** Find out how the audience feels about issues, procedures, or any other pertinent data, and then address it later in the webinar. Figure 2-2 shows a sample survey.
- **Pop quiz:** Test their knowledge on topics or issues.
- **Vote:** Let them vote on matters that range from future meetings to where to hold the office holiday party.
- **Feedback:** Gather information regarding their feedback on the webinar, and use the data to improve future sessions.

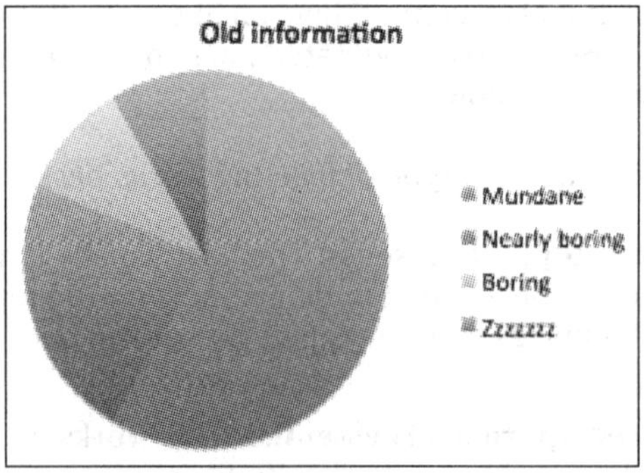

Figure 2-2: A survey.

Selecting the Talent

When you think about it, a webinar doesn't differ that much from an unscripted television show. The goal of each fills some void in an individual's quest for information or curiosity using a loosely structured format that occasionally strives for spontaneity, while at the same time mildly entertaining its audience. To accomplish this task, each requires a team of people to facilitate each part of the production.

Webinars require a small team of people, but due to various constraints, namely budget, most team members have to take on more than one job. That means that the same person can wear multiple hats, with at least one of those hats being managing the online environment.

In the next few sections, I take a look at the stars of the webinar.

Moderator

If you were at a comedy club, this role is equivalent to the emcee. Sometimes it's the same person as the host, but always the one who keeps the webinar running smoothly. The moderator usually introduces the presenter and the speakers. In addition, as the name *moderator* implies, he can lead a moderated panel of several speakers. It's not much different than Jim Lehrer, who is the executive editor of *PBS NewsHour*, moderating the first of the 2012 presidential debates.

At times, the moderator acts as a technical assistant, allowing the presenter to focus on delivering the presentation. This role increases with larger webinars. In addition, this person ensures the experience is optimized for online attendees and will deliver an enjoyable experience that supports repeat attendance.

For the talking part of the job, consider the following:

- **Use your natural speaking voice:** People relate to a clearly spoken regular voice as opposed to someone pretending to be Ron Burgundy. So stay classy, web moderator, stay classy.
- **Check out other moderators:** Be a webinar connoisseur by registering for some different ones. Consider it less about checking out the competition and more as an observation of how others do it. It's a great way to get a sense of communicating in this new medium.
- **Watch talk shows on television:** Don't seek to imitate them, but do become familiar with the conversational style you'll need for moderating an entertaining webinar.
- **Listen to your own voice:** This also helps you improve at public speaking. Listening to your recorded voice helps you grow exponentially. If you've done a webinar in the past, go back and listen to it again. Also, record your voice on your smart phone to get comfortable with public speaking.
- **Join Toastmasters:** This non-profit organization (Figure 2-3) is dedicated to developing public speaking and leadership skills through practice and feedback. Visit their website at `www.toastmasters.org`.

Figure 2-3: The Toastmasters logo.

Presenter

The moderator introduces the webinar and can also moderate it too, but it's the host or presenter (the terms are used interchangeably) who acts as the face of the webinar. Let's think for a moment of a TV variety show. The presenter's role is not quite to yell, "Heeeere's Johnny!" but then again, it's not that much different either. (On the off-chance you're not sure of the reference, it's how *The Tonight Show* sidekick Ed McMahon would introduce Johnny Carson every night.)

You can loosely consider McMahon and his predecessors as moderators. If Johnny Carson was before your time, maybe Jimmy Fallon is a better example. Fallon comes out, does a monologue of current events, and then introduces his guests. Each guest is interviewed and tells something about the movie, television show, or new album. Figure 2-4 shows the presenter addressing his audience.

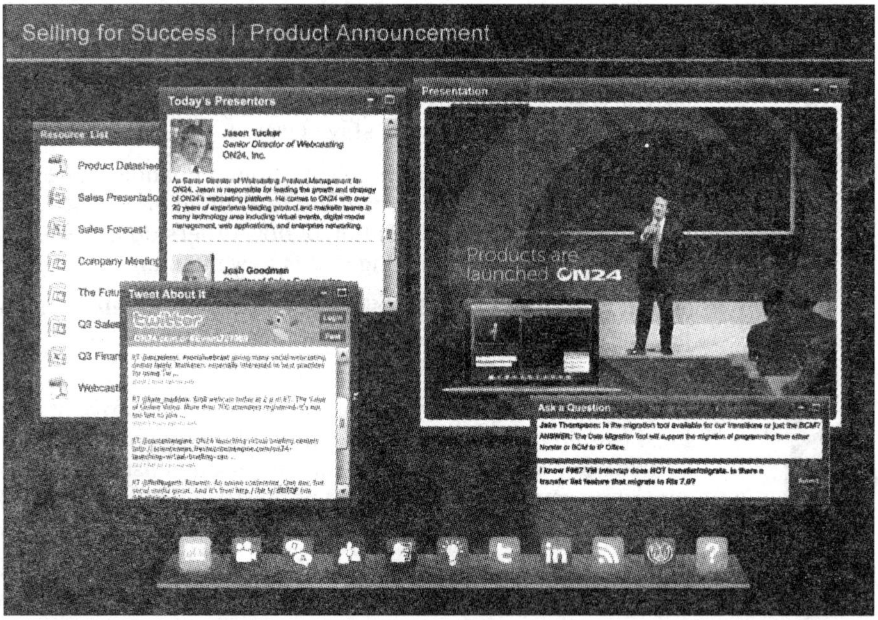

Figure 2-4: This composite image shows a presenter addressing the audience.

Courtesy of ON24

Guest speaker

Don't you just love it when your favorite talk show has a guest whom you really want to see? It gives you something to look forward to and provides a face to the information you're about to find out about their latest movie, new album, or upcoming wedding. Well, guest speakers at a webinar can also generate that kind of excitement.

In its own way, a webinar can offer the same thrill to the viewer by providing expert or celebrity speakers to enhance the discussion. These include various experts, officials, and even celebrities. Special guest speakers attract registrants much like a cool guest on a talk show makes you want to tune in.

Webinars can provide that sense of personality, both with guests and topics that not only share their particular brand of expertise, but also have appeal to your potential audience. Guest can include the following:

- **Entertainment celebrities:** A recognizable actor or musician speaking at the webinar, on its panel, or endorsing a product or service.
- **Industry celebrities:** One of those "rock stars" who is actually not a rock star. Larry Ellison of Oracle comes to mind.

Be entertaining

Here's a widespread misconception: Webinars are simply slide shows with a voiceover track. That description makes the webinar sound devoid of personality, like some modern-day version of those films in junior high school on topics like *Your Body and You*. Come to think of it, some of those were quite funny, although I'm not sure they were supposed to be.

Don't let that your webinar meet that same fate. A webinar can deliver its message while at the same time engaging its audience, but that begins in the planning stage, and then evolves with good writing and the right presenter. Be funny, spin touching narratives, and inject your passion into every part of your presentation. No matter how far-flung your audience, there is simply no substitute for a human connection, even on the web.

Here's what you need to know:

- **Make sure you're prepared:** Know the key points of the meeting and be careful if you decide to improvise, especially if you have a slide-heavy presentation. Make sure you understand the intent of the webinar, as well as the goal of each of its sections.
- **Don't dawdle:** Webinars have a limited time, so your job is to introduce and discuss the topics, as well as have the program move along. Be sure to focus on key points of the meeting and stick to the script.
- **Use analogies:** Sometimes it's easy to explain complex situations by comparing them to everyday situations. For example, here's an analogy for you: On *The Price Is Right*, host Drew Carey does the job of presenter, while announcer George Gray acts as the moderator.

- **High-level experts:** One of the field's leading experts commenting or verifying a product, service, or trend.
- **Politicians:** Either to endorse, to provide insight on a topic, or to say a few words before introducing a guest or speaker.
- **Testimonials:** An individual who endorses a product based on her personal experience.

Structuring the Webinar

Can you imagine watching a movie where the first part that you see is the end? Or perhaps the movie spends a ton of time setting up the plot, and then hurries to finish it so quickly that you missed it if you blinked? That would not be a good movie. The same can be said about a webinar that follows that dark path. Great moments in webinar production share much with an effective story. Each uses a similar structure to introduce the topics, explain it with more detail, and then arrive at a conclusion. In its simplest form, a story is all about grabbing the audience and taking them for a ride.

Like a finely crafted story, your webinar should explain its purpose in the beginning, including the topics and what the audience can expect. Those points are then expressed in the middle with more detail. The last section summarizes the discussed topics, and then is followed by a question-and-answer period. That structure seems simple, but it's how you present the topics in each of those sections that determine the impact of the meeting.

So to recap:

- **Opening:** Here the presenter or moderator explains the topic, discusses the format, and talks about the program's speakers. Think of it as a similar to a talk show host's monologue, only maybe not as funny. It serves as an overview of things to come.
- **Body:** Here's where the presenter delves into each topic and supports the discussion with visual assets like PowerPoint slides, images, and video. Guests are also introduced to discuss different points, be interviewed, or take part in a moderated panel.
- **Close:** The host or moderator summarizes the topics, takes questions, and reaches out for feedback.

Gauging the size of your audience

How many people are you looking to reach? Is it ten? A thousand? Your message stays the same regardless of the size of your audience, but it's always helpful to know how many people are out there taking part in your webinar, and to some degree, to know something about the people logging on.

Before you can count them, you need to get people to log on, so how do you do that? There are many way to promote your webinar, but staying in touch with your potential audience is equally important. You always want repeat participants.

After reaching out and getting potential participants to register, don't expect them all to show up on the day of your webinar. Industry benchmark data show that approximately 45 percent of registrants actually log in to the webinar. Although that's a bit disconcerting, understanding the ratio helps you predict the approximate size of your audience. In addition, their profile information (which you gather when they register) can help you understand their level of knowledge on the topic and qualify them as leads.

Consider the following:

- **Announce early:** Get word out about your webinar as early as possible to maximize the number of people that will register.
- **Confirm registration:** After they sign up, be sure to send them a confirmation e-mail with updates on the program. Acknowledging them also makes them feel connected to you.
- **Send out reminders:** This helps them remember as the dates draws near. The world has gotten busier and sometimes people get distracted and simply forget.
- **Provide practical advice:** Suggest that they do a system test in advance to assure that their connection is working properly. Platform providers usually offer such testing capability.
- **Stay in touch:** Send reminders before the webinar and follow up afterwards with thank-you notes and feedback requests.

Determining the proper length

60 Minutes is not just a popular news program: It's also the optimal time for most webinars. No, not Sunday nights at 7 p.m., but 60 minutes in length. That time works for several reasons, but the attention span of your potential audience is high on the list.

Modern technology with all of its creature comforts and conveniences has led to a much busier lifestyle than that of previous generations. The technology is great for maximizing our time, but not so great when it comes to allowing us to absorb it all. That comes with a price. Research shows our increased activity in people's daily lives has led to a shorter attention span.

That level of attentiveness diminishes further when we're plunked down in front of a computer screen. Why? Because that time online is often divided between checking e-mail, using social media, and playing Candy Crush, all while eating lunch. It's easy to see how the Internet has at least partly supplanted the TV, with us being able to watch it, eat, and do something else at the same time. So along comes that all-day webinar on understanding the latest version of Microsoft Office, and you get almost as excited as you would about watching a congressional filibuster on C-SPAN.

Maybe an all-day training session delivered via the webinar has value, but you'd be hard-pressed to make that argument for a marketing presentation. That's when that pesky axiom "Less is more" comes to mind.

So although 60 minutes is a perfect timeframe for a webinar, you can go slightly longer or shorter to fit your content. Try to *never* go less than 20 minutes. Otherwise, people may not even bother to log on, never mind the fact that you won't be able to get enough information to your audience in that short period of time.

Deciding how much is too much

When Bruce Springsteen performs in concert, he gives the audience their money's worth not just by playing an intense set, but also by playing longer than many other artists do. Although that quality is fantastic in a concert, webinar audiences are not as receptive toward a lengthy session.

Instead, your webinar needs to provide your audience with enough material to let them fully understand the topic, but not so much that you overload them with information until their brains hurt. If that happens, they'll eventually need a time out or simply lose interest and log off before the webinar is done. The same applies when you don't provide enough information, or when you gloss over key parts of the discussion.

Striking the right balance is truly an art form that depends on quickly getting each point on your agenda across to your audience, while at the same time remembering that your goal is to keep them interested and entertained.

Back in school, you probably had a teacher who kept you interested while at the same time moving class along briskly. Then compare him to those messengers of the mundane who seemed to drone on and on. Those droners probably drove their students to doing homework for other classes or some hardcore doodling.

The same holds true for the webinar when a participant loses interest. When boredom strikes, the participant probably checks his e-mail, updates Facebook, or texts his friends. And yes, the situation can get even worse if your participants start mocking you via text message or Twitter.

Creating an agenda

Just as an NFL coach plans a complex strategy for an upcoming game, or a law student studies different topics for the bar exam, the success of a webinar depends on having a clearly structured agenda.

Conversely, if you haphazardly run your meeting, chances are that some topics will run longer or shorter than allotted, and ultimately some key subject would go under-discussed. When you miss delivering critical points within each section, it can diminish the webinar's effectiveness. That, in turn, translates into a waste of time for your audience.

REMEMBER

Having an agenda simply allows you to allocate the proper amount of time for each section. Although it's merely a list of topics and discussion points for the meeting, it creates a more cohesive experience that hopefully will promote discussion when it comes to implementing new policies, understanding new procedures, or introducing a new product, because that, after all, is the goal of any meeting. Besides, it's better than the contrary: having your participants lose of an hour of their lives they'll never get back.

Here are some aspects to consider for your agenda:

TIP

- **Yes, you need one:** Whether it's a quarterly progress meeting, an information session on the rollout for a new dependent care policy in the workplace, or the launch of a new tablet device that comes in a new shape, make sure you have an agenda for presenting it.
- **Keep it relevant:** If you want to keep your audience engaged, be sure the topics are relevant to everyone who is logged on.
- **Take suggestions:** Reach out to your audience before the webinar to gauge their interest in topics for the meeting.
- **Know your topics ahead of time:** If you want to sound like an expert, don't assume it happens from staying at a Holiday Inn Express. Instead, try to understand the topic and subject matter. Remember, if participants smell incompetence, they will not stick around.
- **Have an alert team:** Because your support staff needs to focus on the webinar, urge them to pay attention and to refrain from using their cell phones or making fantasy football trades while it's going on.

Having all your content ready

We've all heard about the virtues of preparation since childhood. You know: Do your homework, study for tests, and don't wait until the night before it's due to begin your science fair project. Then there are the more practical prep tips like packing your school bag and laying out your clothes the night before.

That last one is important because although you can watch a webinar in your underwear, presenting one in your skivvies is frowned-upon. Putting that aside, you should have everything prepared in its entirety from the first rehearsal. That means you should write your script, gather your slides (after gathering figures and making sure all of your information is correct), and channel the energy of being seen by an enormous crowd.

Because you cannot read your audience's faces, you better make sure your writing is witty and informative and your charm is dead-on (but more on that later). Your words to the audience are enhanced by slides of images, graphics, and buzzwords that help get your point across. So after you have a rough script in place, begin to compile your content, because the success of your webinar depends on it.

Making sure time is properly allocated

Say you were running a webinar for your fantasy football buddies on the upcoming season, and you scheduled it for 60 minutes. Then you divided it into four 15-minute sections and called them quarters, you know, just like in an NFL game.

If you did that and promised to talk about a few specific examples in each quarter, you'd better make sure there's enough time to cover everything you promised. Otherwise, you wouldn't deliver on what was promised and your buddies would leave the webinar unfulfilled. The same holds true for a webinar audience, except for the fact that maybe unlike your buddies, they won't wait around if the information promised does not properly progress.

Remember, if people take the time out of their busy days for your webinar, you had better make sure that each section runs on time and fulfills what was promised. Otherwise, your reputation will suffer and registration will most likely decline the next time you run a webinar.

Consider the following:

- **Rehearse the show:** Make sure your words coincide with the slides.
- **Pace yourself:** Don't rush or slow down during the webinar. Take your time and stay on point.
- **Stick to the script:** Maybe you don't have to follow it word for word, but enough that each section of the webinar runs smoothly.

Deciding between free or fee

On any given day, users can troll the web and find a host of free webinars covering a far range of topics. Most of them are free, last around an hour, and provide an overview of the topic. That begs the question: To pay, or not to pay? The answer is not always a simple one. Sometimes, the answer is apparent. For example, few people would consider paying for a webinar on health plans. Conversely, users would plunk down a few bucks on a training session for certification on a new software application. Fee-based webinars generally appeal to the user looking for an elevated level of content or education. Many cover subject areas that users would normally pay to attend in a physical space.

Another use for a fee-based webinar takes place when people cannot attend a fee-based seminar that takes place in a physical location either because they cannot make it that day or it's sold out. Fee-based webinars attract fewer registrants than free ones, but there's another interesting statistic. In the paid arena, registration runs around 90 percent as opposed to the 45 percent (according to ON24) in the free version. Experts attribute this to trend to various reasons, including that registrants sign up because they have to attend as part of a job requirement or training need. On the free side, a lot of people who are interested when they see the registration page don't always follow through. The decision to offer your webinar for fee or free strongly depends on what you have to offer and the demand.

Chapter 3

Putting Together a Webinar Team

In This Chapter

- Identifying webinar production roles
- Understanding the types of audiences
- Treating the audience right

The old adage of there being no "I" in team remains true, although there *is* an "I" in *webinar.* Whether related to work, art, or recreation, the team concept often turns "one into fun." Everything from playing baseball to making movies demands a team effort. For example, our nation's favorite pastime needs nine players on each side to play a regulation game, and a film production needs a director, cinematographer, and actors to make it work.

But anyone who has ever brought a bat and ball to the playground or a camcorder along for a ride with some friends knows that you can always improvise with less. That's good, because webinars often demand a bigger team than usually is available, so most of the time, they're scaled down to a few people if not one person running it. Taking a page from the playground, the webinar often requires each person involved to take on multiple roles, so depending on the size of the webinar, you might have a full team, or more than likely, the abridged schoolyard version.

The first step to webinar bliss has little to do with the technology, and more about figuring out the pieces and how they all fit together. That begins with the players.

Getting to Know the People in Your Webinar

REMEMBER

How many people does it take to run a webinar? If this were a riddle, here's the likely answer: "At least one person, but ideally, many more than you actually have." Not much different than a motion picture production, webinars have a producer on top to run the operation, talent on the floor, and a support staff that helps it comes together. But that's where the similarities end because instead of a support army, it's often a force of one (or sometimes two or three) getting the job done.

One individual can perform a basic webinar, but will wear many hats during the process. Figure 3-1 shows users setting up a webinar. Of course, bigger webinars require more people wearing fewer hats. With that said, the average webinar team consists of three people, including a moderator, presenter, and other support roles. How many people and how many hats they wear depends on the actual size and scope of the event.

REMEMBER

Never forget the most important person in your webinar: the attendee. The more you understand about the folks you're reaching out to, the better you can serve them.

In the next few sections, I examine the roles of everyone in the webinar production process.

Figure 3-1: Setting up the webinar.

The producer

If you enjoy puzzles, as seen in Figure 3-2, thrive on making a whole from the sum of parts, or bringing order to chaos, the role of webinar producer will fit you like a custom-made glove. Making it all come together is what a webinar producer does every time. Perched atop the planning universe, the producer plots the course for the webinar, dodges obstacles, and puts out fires along the way.

Whether you're bold enough to do it yourself or you're looking for a service to run your company's next online session, the producer creates the entire event. Responsibilities include doing everything necessary for putting the webinar together, from getting leads for potential registrants and writing the script to marketing the session and running it. In addition, the producer leads the team and can even moderate.

Every aspect of the webinar falls under this title. The producer makes all kind of decisions, including things like deciding exactly when to broadcast the webinar for maximum potential. (Believe it or not, there is a prime time for a webinar broadcast. That's something that's often goes unnoticed, yet it can determine the success of running a webinar. See the "Timing is everything" sidebar for more on that.)

REMEMBER

The producer needs to take all of the components of the show — the topic, talent, and platform provider — and cohesively produce the webinar piece-by-piece. That responsibility includes getting leads on potential registrants, marketing the webinar, and then actually making sense of the webinar in the best way to tell the story. Keep in mind that all this usually needs to happen in a relatively short amount of time.

Figure 3-2: A webinar producer puts all the pieces together, much like a puzzle.

Sometimes a webinar producer acts as a "gun for hire," working for external clients. For example, a company may be familiar with running webinars, but not with the service or software, so a provider can supply a producer to the company's team to help. That producer would be contracted out.

So to recap, the responsibilities of the producer include

REMEMBER

- **Planning the webinar:** Holds meetings in the early stages to flesh out ideas and translate them to presentation.
- **Putting the team together:** Selects the speakers, guests, and support staff, and trains them, if necessary.
- **Marketing the webinar:** Gets the word out to potential participants using e-mail, social media, and other marketing techniques, as seen in Figure 3-3.
- **Uploading the presentation:** Makes sure that presentation is uploaded correctly into the webinar host software and that all the pieces are present and correct, such as software settings and widgets. The producer also makes sure that any extra plug-ins or features (polls, surveys, and so on) are all pointing to the right places. All this TLC makes the user experience as smooth as possible.
- **Moderating if necessary:** Sometimes the producer moderates the webinar; other times, the producer finds the right person for the job.

Figure 3-3: A marketing graphic or notice.

Timing is everything

The actual time when you present your content often is as important as the content itself. According to webinar service provider ON24, as seen in the following figure, there's a significant difference in registration numbers when scheduling a webinar at 10 a.m. on a Tuesday morning as opposed to doing it at 3 p.m. on the Friday before a holiday weekend. With all things being equal, which of them would you attend? And if you choose the latter, would you pay attention as carefully as you would to a webinar on an average Tuesday?

The moderator

Not many job descriptions are as direct as this one is. Think about it: How many of us know exactly what a phlebotomist, actuary, or sous-chef really does? Probably not many, but we *all* know that a moderator moderates. In other words, the moderator makes sure that the webinar runs as planned.

Using the TV production equivalent, put it in perspective. *Saturday Night Live* announcer Don Pardo announces the cast, host, and musical guest star every week for the show. *The Price Is Right* announcer George Gray announces the show, calls contestants, and introduces prizes along with the show's host, Drew Carey, who can be thought of as its presenter (more on that in the next section).

The responsibility of the moderator encompasses a variety of roles that range from setting the scene, introducing the presentation, and sometimes taking questions during the Q&A portion of the program. A moderator must have a well-rounded knowledge of webinar structure along with an understanding of the content, or at least an effective way to present it.

But there's another important quality that the moderator must also possess: impeccable organizational skills. That order keeps the entire operation moving ahead and engaging the audience.

On the communication side, there's the virtue of having a good speaking voice. If George Gray, *The Price Is Right* announcer, were replaced by a less-trained voice, would it still grab your attention? What if it was a voice that sounded like Rocky Balboa, or maybe Bullwinkle's flying squirrel pal, Rocky? After the initial chuckles, would you take it seriously? (Okay, maybe you *would* take Rocket J. Squirrel seriously, but just for old time's sake.) Without a clear and concise voice, it's hard to understand what a moderator is saying.

So although a Don Pardo-type voice might be overkill (but very cool at the same time), a moderator needs to speak with conviction. Besides, the moderator doesn't really talk for the entire webinar, but he does need to set up the essential part of the show.

Here are the necessary qualities of the moderator:

- **Introducing the webinar:** Somewhere between "Live from New York!" and "Come on dowww-nnnn" lies the right style for welcoming guests to the webinar.
- **Keeping the session moving smoothly:** Announces each section or part of the webinar, making sure each runs on time.
- **Moderating a panel of guests:** For moderated discussions, the webinar moderator often introduces the panels, sets up the topics, and plays traffic cop in case things get unruly.

The presenter

If the moderator must possess a good speaking voice, what kind of golden throat are you expecting from the presenter? One that's equally good will suffice, but a presenter also needs an engaging screen presence and subject matter expertise.

Although a dynamic personality is always a plus, the presenter, as seen in Figure 3-4, often has a much greater role besides being the face of the operation. Long before the webinar broadcasts online, or is even promoted, the presenter's job begins early in the process, shaping topics and goals discussed in a meeting room, fleshing out the important stuff.

Figure 3-4: A webinar presenter.

Wearing the hat of writer for the program, the presenter prepares content, translating key points and building slides for the PowerPoint portion of the program.

On show day, the presenter is front and center discussing the webinar content.

Here's a summary of what the presenter does:

- **Organizes the content:** Looks for key phrases, talking points, and slides to maximize time efficiency and information value.
- **Writes the presentation:** If she doesn't write the entire presentation, she at least puts together some rough version of the main points of the session. The good presenters tell jokes, whereas the great ones entertain and inform their audience.
- **Speaks clearly:** Few things are more annoying than a talking head no one can understand.

The director

Webinars require direction, but smaller ones don't have a separate director. Whether it's the producer wearing another hat, or a separate person directing the action, webinars on a large scale benefit from a director. Usually, that distinction depends on whether the webinar relies heavily on video, especially when multiple camera setups are used. Most of the time, the producer directs the webinar from behind the scenes. The exception is when there's video involved. In that case, a separate director is needed to make sure the subject is properly guided.

The tech team

Depending on the size of your webinar, you can handle the tech issues yourself, have a helper, or use a full team to pull it off. Regardless of the size of your team, expect to work hard to make it an impressive webinar.

TIP

The idea of running an interactive meeting over the web sounds easy, yet many things can go wrong during the presentation. You may experience audio problems, the slides may not refresh on the screen, or the broadcast might drop out completely. These issues need to be quickly resolved, or it's your audience that drops out next.

Then there's the live Q&A. It's impractical to expect the presenter to vet each question along with taking on his other duties. It's nice to have someone dedicated to that task go through the questions that come in at that part of the webinar. Sometimes the moderator can pull it off; at other times, a specific individual is dedicated to dealing with it.

The promoter

Whether you plan to promote your own webinar or want to delegate that responsibility to someone else, the promoter helps put "butts in seats." (Of course, those seats are in front of their computer screens.) The ideal candidate needs to understand how to drive registration, attendance, and on-demand viewing. The ability to write a compelling invitation along with social media savvy are necessary skills, if you want maximum attendance.

Getting to Know Your Audience

REMEMBER

There's no denying the role that familiarity plays in strengthening a relationship. Whether it's your future best friend, new colleague, or life partner, the better you understand them, the more equipped you are to know where they are coming from. Simply multiply that idea by several hundred to several thousand, and you'll have some idea what it takes to acquaint your audience with what you have to offer by understanding what they need. Remember that Michael Keaton film, *Multiplicity*? It's the one where his character is copied into multiple versions of himself. Well, you don't have to go to that extreme, but here are a few things that can help.

The main aspect to consider about the average webinar, as seen from the viewer's perspective in Figure 3-5, is that its audience comes from every walk of life. That makes it necessary to understand the flavor of each user type, from customers and business partners to students and employees.

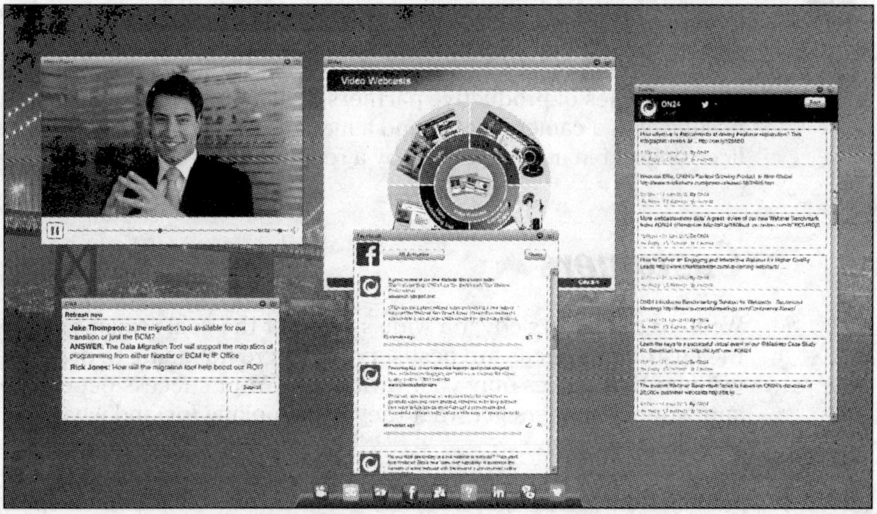

Figure 3-5: How a viewer sees the webinar from home.

Here are some things your team must do for your audience:

- **Communicate with them:** Use polls and surveys to get to know their needs and desires before, during, and after the webinar. Also, read their feedback and try to respond, when possible.
- **Take action over their concerns:** As the wants and needs of your prospective audience as well as the market trends of the industry become clear, you can adapt to better serve their needs.
- **Solve their problem:** Have a clear idea of the problem that your targeted audience faces and provide solutions that attract them.
- **Use their jargon:** Mention last night's baseball match or controversial decision by the local NFL team's manager to a sports fan and expect them to politely change the conversation after rolling their eyes. (Baseball has games, not matches, and NFL teams have coaches, not managers.) Using the wrong terminology is a dead giveaway that you don't know what you're talking about. Nobody has the time to listen to

someone who is out of touch, especially when they're not speaking the proper lingo when reaching out to a prospective audience. Get the terminology just right by making the proper word choices and tone when it comes to inviting them.

Partners

Your strategic partners and affiliates play a role in your webinar team because when things go right, everyone looks good. Besides helping promote the session, your partners can also provide content for the webinar, suggest or supply appropriate speakers, or just provide a little extra clout. In addition, you can motivate your partners with incentives based on the documented referrals they bring in. But often, the webinar benefits the partners in some way. Examples of productive partnerships include a webinar on DSLR moviemaking with a camera maker and a media card manufacturer, or a real estate licensing webinar put together by a realtor and a real estate attorney.

Customers

Webinar customers cover a wide swath yet the goal remains the same: that the customer's needs are best served. You're not going to draw them in for a webinar that serves only your own needs. Your success depends on making sure your customers get what they were looking for, and what you have promised to them.

Your customer is a valued member of your team. Think about sports analogies like the tenth man in baseball, and the twelfth man in football. The webinar has an average of three team members, so . . . I'm not sure whether that makes the customer the fourth man, but you get the idea.

When you do right by your audience, they will most certainly do right by you. If you don't waste their time and pummel them with the digital version of junk, they will keep coming back.

Here are some traits that you can hope they exhibit:

- **Follows through:** You hope that not only do they register for the webinar, but they also show up. Statistics show that 45 percent of registrants actually attend.
- **Stays for it all:** Some folks sign on to a webinar and drop out sometime after it starts and before it ends. The ideal participant stays for the entire webinar.

- **Remains an active participant:** Asks questions during the Q&A period, downloads content and fills out polls and surveys.
- **Name-drops your webinar:** Will mention in casual conversation and via social channels the value of your webinar, how it benefitted them, and how it may impact others.

Webinar registrants can also help promote the webinar through a variety of ways, including posting on social media as well as the time-honored word of mouth. You can proactively ask them to tell a friend. Often, this sort of endorsement has more power than anything else you can try.

Understanding the Types of Audiences

Participants come to your webinar in all shapes and sizes, but with the same goal: to get something valuable out of that 60 minutes spent sitting in front of their computer screen. Webinar content/attendees/objectives are all based on meeting audience needs. To understand their importance as your audience, it's helpful understanding their role in coming each time.

Here are a few audience types to consider:

- **Customers:** The webinar producer plans content around existing customers (for example, a user conference).
- **Prospects:** Arguably the number one type of webinar because most webinars are hosted by marketers and are designed for lead generation.
- **Employees:** Sometimes they're part of your company or organization, whereas other times, they work for someone else. It's all good because employees, as seen in Figure 3-6, make up a large segment of the webinar viewing audience. Whether it's learning about the company's new health plan, understanding the newest features of the latest version of SAP, or training on new procedures, it's essential to give them what they need.
- **Learners:** Word of mouth applies to learners too. Give them a great experience, and they will often return and tell their friends. Give them what they need to know. For trainees, it's important to provide something they need to learn or can get certified in. The key thing is content and relevancy of content. If I want to get certified in some particular software, and you're offering a webinar about something else, I probably won't be interested. It's about making sure your content is relevant to your audience.

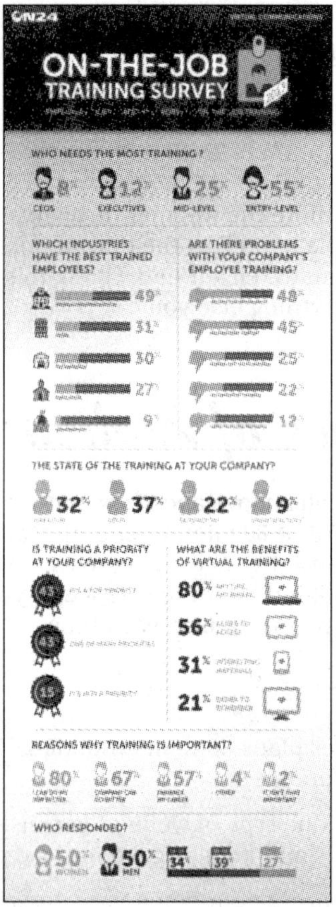

Figure 3-6: An on-the-job training survey graphic.

Part II
Preparing an Effective Webinar

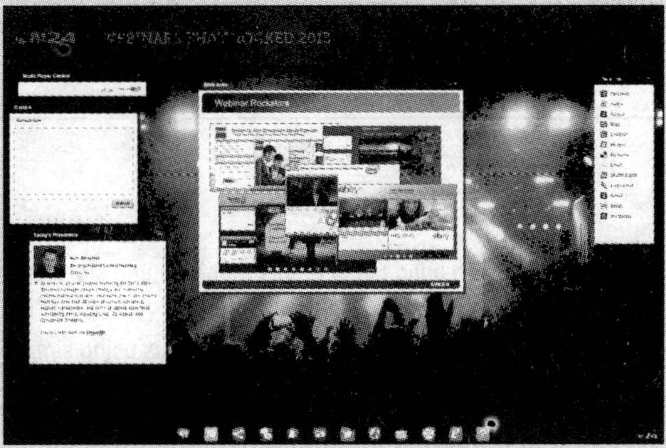

web extras

Visit `www.dummies.com` for a look at seminars now and then.

In this part . . .

- Understand how to build Excel tables that hold and store the data you need to analyze.
- Find quick and easy ways to begin your analysis using simple statistics, sorting, and filtering.
- Get practical stratagems and commonsense tactics for grabbing data from extra sources.
- Discover tools for cleaning and organizing the raw data you want to analyze.

Chapter 4

Choosing a Platform

In This Chapter

- Deciding what level of service you want
- Getting audience support
- Finding the right provider for your budget

Selecting the right webinar platform is a little bit like picking out the right pair of shoes. The selection is vast, and just because you find your usual size doesn't mean it's the best fit. It's not much different when you're searching for someone to help put on your webinar. As these interactive online events grow in popularity, new vendors, platforms, and providers are springing up quicker than weeds coming up through the bricks on my front walk. That's why it's important to find the one that works best for you — just like finding the most stylish and most comfortable shoes.

If Goldilocks were looking to do a webinar on the art of finding the perfect bed-and-breakfast, surely she would think about mattress comfort and porridge temperature, and maybe even cover places to stumble upon when roaming through the woods.

It's the same when it comes to picking a platform that you think is right for your needs. That's because webinar services range from do-it-yourself to near-concierge service (also called *white glove service*), and they cost anywhere from nothing (or next to nothing) to an annual cost comparable buying a luxury automobile. You may require more or less, depending on your needs.

Webinars are usually live events, so reliability is very important. Not being properly supported by a provider or presenters becomes the number one stumbling block. There's nothing worse than having a problem five minutes before you go to air, and nobody responds to your message asking for help. Although there are many capable providers, it all comes down to your confidence in delivery, both yours in the presentation, and the provider's ability to run it as promised.

So what exactly do you need to accomplish your next webinar? That answer obviously depends on what you have to say and how many people you want to tell. But more specifically, it depends on how much control you want or need over the presentation.

Deciding Between Self-Service and Full-Service

Sometimes you want to eat in a restaurant where a gentleman dressed much like the penguin as seen in Figure 4-1 serves you everything you desire at a whim. Other times, you feel like picking up a tray and making your way through a long buffet line. Whatever you decide depends on your needs and budget at the time. It's the same for choosing a webinar level of service.

If you're tech-savvy and have a manageable plan for your webinar, you may want to do it yourself. Other times, you'll relish the value of the webinar equivalent of that penguin that served you earlier. It all depends on the situation, but consider this advice: When it comes to external audiences, there should be nothing that limits your reach to them — not geographical boundaries, time zones, or technology.

The first two — geography and time zones — are clearly out of your control, but when it comes to the latter, there's a wide list of issues to consider to make sure your message gets out to the audience. These range from cross-platform device support to making sure the user is familiar with the webinar tools.

Figure 4-1: The penguin some waiters aspire to dress like.

Exploring self-service

Can you run your webinar yourself? More than likely, the answer is yes. Here's why. When you're a presenter dialing in to a telephony system, or using your webcam, you can usually do that by yourself, especially for small to medium presentations. There's no need for your webinar provider to do anything. Most providers sell subscription packages for those who want to handle their webinar themselves to reach their audience

TIP

On the other hand, if you get into a more complex situation where, for example, your presenter is on stage at the convention center, and you need a camera crew out there, you're going to need to tap into a provider's full-service options. You can still run it yourself, but you may warrant some help.

There's a perception that a webinar can require a lot of help to pull it off. A DIY solution like ON24's Webcast Elite is easy-to-use and requires minimal support, but not all webinar providers are created equal. You want one that can train you and help you to run it yourself without a hitch, but that offers help just a phone call away if you get into trouble.

REMEMBER

By doing it by yourself, you clearly reduce the number of heads needed to put it on. For example, the producer and moderator, or maybe the presenter and the moderator, are often the same person. Often, these self-service presentations have a single person moderating, presenting, and managing the Q&A. That means you can even run the entire webinar from your desktop in front of your computer.

Going full-service

The alternative to staying at a roadside motel for the night and eating pizza you bring back to the room for dinner is checking into a luxury hotel in a big room with a real down comforter on the bed, and then having room service bring you lobster and a glass of champagne as seen in Figure 4-2. Self-service gets the job done, but full-service provides much more support, fewer worries, and more comfort.

REMEMBER

A full-service provider offers peace of mind because every part of the webinar is done for you. That means you get access to numerous features and have a team backing you when it comes to training and monitoring the presentation. Sometimes they even moderate the event. All you have to do is supply the content. And if you're not comfortable speaking, they can even provide a professional speaker for you. A typical package provides help in the background, but generally you do it all yourself, and seek assistance when needed.

Figure 4-2: Waiter about to serve glasses of champagne.

Keeping technology out of the way

Technology is a funny thing. When you really understand how it works, it makes your life easier. And when you don't quite get it, the feeling of being stuck in a traffic jam that never moves comes to mind. Someone who lacks tech savvy may find joining and attending an online event a little scary. This differs from a physical seminar, where participants need to do no more than meander into a large room, sit down, and listen. It's also different from a mandatory internal employee webinar where everyone logs on and help is rarely more than a cubicle away.

Marketing an external webinar is a different ballgame. If the registration process or console is too complicated, a user can say: "Well, that's one click too many, so I'm gone."

That's why it's important to choose a provider that has a track record for a happy user experience. Be weary of providers that require participants to download additional plug-ins. Remember, many companies have firewalls, so employees may be unable to download anything.

Managing interaction between the roles

Think of every webinar as having three roles. There's a producer — that's the person that sets it up, designs the registration page, and does all that kind of work. Then there's the presenter or presenters. This person hosts the event, runs the web console, and controls the PowerPoint presentation. And then, of course, there's the participant who is on the receiving end, better known as your potentially adoring public. All three of these roles must interact as flawlessly as possible to maintain a high level of engagement. Each should concentrate on their own roles — even if it's the same person wearing all the hats — so having a comfortable experience with your webinar provider makes life a little easier.

Evaluating your needs for a partner

Sometimes your webinar provider acts as your partner, at least in terms of getting your message out to the masses. Besides support and stability, here are some other crucial items to consider when finding a partner to reach out to an external audience.

They include

- **Customization and flexibility:** It's important for your webinar interface to reflect the best look for your webinar so it represents your organization positively. Customizing your webinar console quickly is one important aspect.
- **Leads, leads, leads:** The questions of getting the best leads and answering the following questions. What's my cost per lead? How am I going to qualify those leads? How am I going to get those leads in front of my sales people quickly and effectively? A partner that can deliver more leads is a true partner, indeed.
- **Platform analytics:** The platform must play a role as a source of data and as a data collection tool. That includes information from polling, recording Q&A, and the ability to monitor chat.

Shopping Around

Although there are many webinar providers out there, determining the right one for your needs more often than not comes down to budget. Figuring out exactly what you need from a webinar becomes an important part of the equation. For example, if you want to reach an audience of one hundred people or fewer, you can choose from some inexpensive options to keep your costs down. Obviously, the more participants you expect at your webinar, the greater your needs from the provider. That's why it's necessary to shop for a webinar provider as you would shop for anything else, as seen in Figure 4-3.

REMEMBER

For anywhere from close to free (some charges will apply) to a couple of hundred dollars, you can hold a moderate-sized webinar of a couple of hundred people. You probably won't get much in terms of support or customizability, but you can pull it off. From there, the service level climbs to concierge-style support, and the cost increases with the services offered.

Figure 4-3: Shoppers.

Determining what service is right for your needs

Finding the right service provider for your needs shares much in common with dating. To find your perfect match, consider the following:

- **Determine what you need:** Do you want to hold a fully functional, interactive webinar? Or is it more like a big, online meeting? These factors can dramatically affect cost, so be sure you know exactly what you need.

- **Know your budget:** You already know how much money you can spend, so there's no sense is looking at higher-end webinar providers if your budget doesn't allow for it. Many providers charge a monthly fee as part of your contractual obligation, whether you hold a monthly webinar or not. Some allow you to pay as you go. If your needs are basic, you should instead consider using a live meeting service. That may work for your needs. But remember, in webinars as in everything else, you get what you pay for.

TIP

- **Do a trial run:** Or do many of them. Lots of full-service and self-service webinar providers allow users to try out their service for a limited time, usually 30 days. Of course, you're limited to the number of participants you can host and some of the more sophisticated features may not be included in a trial. Each provider will differ in trial features, but at least you can get some idea that way.

Deciding what you need from a provider

Knowing what you need for your webinar is half the battle when it comes to finding the right people to facilitate it. Sometimes that's a little harder than it seems with all different sorts of packages and price structures.

You can narrow it down by determining the following:

- **Needs:** Some users only need to reach a small group of specialized participants, whereas others are attempting to reach a mass audience. Obviously, the latter requires a full-service webinar provider, while the former may suffice with a web meeting service.
- **Objective:** If you want to communicate with large groups, say 500 or more, you need to find a provider that can fully support it. If not, consider the lower-priced online meeting services.
- **Budget:** Some webinars are inexpensive, whereas others can cost thousands of dollars. Clearly, your budget will also dictate your choices, but that doesn't mean you shouldn't try to get the most for your money. When it comes to budget, however, remember: Determining webinar costs is tricky because pricing can vary widely, depending on factors such as volume, audience size, features and technical complexity.
- **Features:** Some providers offer more services than others, whether it's the console, video capability, a phone bridge (that's what facilitates the multi-user call by making each participant punch in a specific code), or numerous other choices. It's a matter of making sure that whomever you choose offers the right combination of features.

Assessing broadcast/webcast capability

REMEMBER

Most webinar providers — and live-meeting services — support video these days. Depending on your needs, some providers are better suited for your webinars than others. Basic video often means broadcasting over a webcam, or maybe an iPad with Retina display under the right lighting. On the upper end of the spectrum, you can expect fully produced video comparable to a television show. Check with potential providers to make sure they're the proper match for what you're trying accomplish.

Getting day-of-webinar support

Technical support on the day of your event is another important requirement when choosing a webinar platform. Not that most don't offer support — it's just that some have a better track record than others.

Because 85 percent of the webinars run on phone bridges, some packages provide a person to monitor the event to assist participants with technical issues. A more elaborate fully managed package may include an on-site crew for technical support, and some even use Skype off-site to assess and fix problems.

In the full-service model, the provider is on the phone with the presenters doing audio checks, the pre-event role, and everything leading up to the event.

REMEMBER

With self-service, technical support is basically available on the other end of the phone line. In a standard case, the customer is operating independently and can call a live event support hotline, in case there's a problem five minutes before.

Getting audience support

REMEMBER

Because webinars are a relatively new concept — at least in the mainstream — not all users have the same ability to understand the technology, even if you send them instructional materials in advance. Some need extra help getting started or assistance if something doesn't work properly during the presentation. Be sure to provide a technical support phone number right on the login screen and console. With a full-service provider, especially with very large presentation, they may provide a support person on-site to immediately address problems. They can field and respond to all of the technical questions that are going on during the webcast and leave only the subject matter questions for the presentation team. Lesser-priced packages can provide service over chat, as seen in Figure 4-4, or through a toll-free number. It's a good idea to ask about audience support when you're selecting your provider.

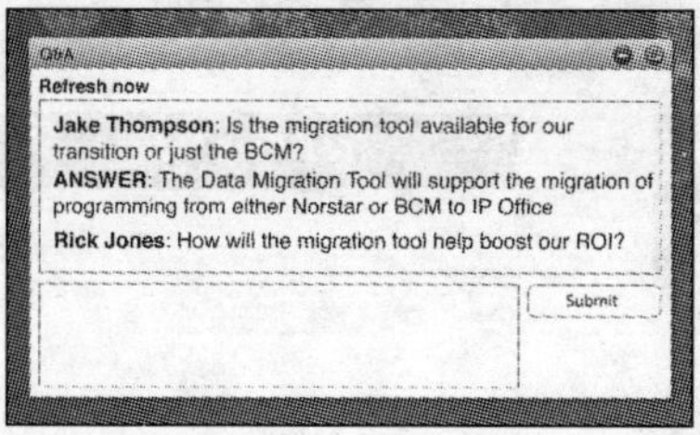

Figure 4-4: Using chat for assistance.

Selecting the Right Kind of Service

Like choosing between fast-food restaurants and fine dining, part of the decision about your webinar provider has to do with how much you can afford or want to spend. Some are affordable enough for a small organization to take advantage of their technology, whereas others provide high-level service at a steep cost. Then there are the freebies; they're not full-fledged webinars, but they can come in handy if your needs are somewhat limited.

Free

The best things in life are free; unfortunately an expansive webinar doesn't usually fall under that category — at least, not on a permanent basis.

TIP

Signing up for a trial run from an established webinar provider, as seen in Figure 4-5, acts as cost-free alternative — at least temporarily. This comes in handy, especially when it comes to learning exactly how well the chosen service runs. Trial periods are generally limited to the number of viewers or features, but you can at least get your feet wet.

The trial doesn't provide a long-term solution — until you start paying, anyway. At least with the webinar trial, you'll have access to the proper tools for conducting it, regardless if it's limited.

Figure 4-5: The sign-up page for a free trial.

On a budget

Discount webinar providers and online meeting services make it possible to hold your presentation online for a fraction of the cost of some full-webinar services, as well as some of the pricier self-service options. Again, however, remember that sometimes you get what you pay for.

If you find a webinar service that fits your needs and budget, by all means go for it. Otherwise, an online meeting service may work for your needs.

WARNING! Online meeting technology is not true event technology, so it has a lot of shortcomings. It doesn't collect the kind of data that a fuller service does by recording and assessing lead qualifications. It doesn't allow much, if any, customization, so you're limited in projecting your brand. For example, you're stuck with their landing page and webinar console look. Video capability is more limited too, so you cannot perform a sophisticated live presentation. It doesn't offer those kinds of features.

Although these services work well for smaller-sized presentations, the collaboration technology when you get above a couple of hundred users starts to come apart for a variety of reasons. If you put a thousand people on the phone all at once and you're paying a dime a minute per user, the costs are going to get out of hand. You don't have to worry about that with true event technology because you're streaming everything.

No limits

When you're a larger organization that produces numerous webinars throughout the year, it's often a good idea to leave the job to the professionals with few hassles. With concierge-style service, all you have to supply is the presenter. The provider does the rest. Often the service includes a project manager that does everything from host the kick-off call to moderate the event. Essentially this level of service manages and executes every detail of the webinar for you.

Service levels rise to include sophisticated television production with post-production in the studio so that they client gets a polished video that they can use as a part of their webcasts. The approach shares a bit more in common with a television network, where you prerecord and edit top quality content and then broadcast that. That kind of service can cost up to tens of thousands of dollars.

Somewhere in the middle

Many webinar producers depend on service at a middle level with a lot of features and support, but few of the extra frills. It's ideal for a medium-sized webinar in the range of a several hundred participants. When you need to step it up with additional services, say increased video capability, these services are generally available for a fee.

One step up from that are advanced service packages. For example, say a company has an event where their CEO is the presenter, but they need a little extra help to make sure all goes right. It's not their routine type of event. For this one, they need extra people to help, maybe to stand by and monitor the event and deal with any technical difficulties on the spot. Sometimes clients subscribe to 20 or 30 events for the year and might upgrade a couple of times to those monitoring packages for special events or maybe for their first couple of events to jump-start their service.

Chapter 5

Planning Your Material

In This Chapter

- Bringing the page to the stage
- Putting a plan together
- Building an outline
- Creating an effective flow
- Interacting with social media
- Using the script to work best for you

If you were a fan of the '80s TV series or the later film *The A-Team*, you'll most likely remember when team leader Col. Hannibal Smith would utter his trademark catchphrase: "I love it when a plan comes together." (He usually said it right after the guys built something out of scrap metal, electronics, and old lumber to thwart whomever was coming after them.)

Everybody loves it when a plan comes together. Unfortunately, it doesn't happen as often as we'd like. Not dedicating enough time to a project or failing to plan it logically tends to be the biggest cause of problems. Other times, we don't bother to think about it much until the last minute. Or worse, we think that a webinar can run itself, and when it fails, we make an excuse along the lines of, "The dog ate my webinar script."

Success and planning go together like a glass of Pinot noir and a mustard-crusted salmon filet, and they're much better than having no plan and winding up with a cold hamburger and a flat cup of soda.

The formula for success is complicated, whereas the recipe for failure is relatively simple. That's because not planning your webinar thoroughly — or failing to seek the proper support — can be a waste of time and money. In turn, it can lead to your audience losing confidence in you the next time around, creating a slippery slope that causes your registration numbers to dwindle in the future.

But that's nothing that a little elbow grease and preparation cannot fix. Remember, poor planning leads to poor production more often than your favorite network drama goes to commercial at the most critical point in the show. But at least in that case, after a bathroom break and a snack, you can pick up where you left off. Regrettably, with a badly planned webinar, the need for a bathroom break may come during the actual presentation, with no return likely.

So whether you're a procrastinator looking for redemption or an organizer searching for that perfect blueprint to success, this chapter shows you how to plan your webinar and hopefully sets you on the path to glory.

Putting It on the Page and on the Stage

Imagine going to the theater to see a play where the actors decided to ignore the script, and not in some cool, groundbreaking improvisational way, either. Imagine instead that they disregarded it completely or chose to perform a play that the playwright never finished. The thread of storytelling would suffer, with the pace, delivery, and outcome being arbitrary to the point of disaster. Perhaps an optimist would deem such a play an avant-garde success, but nobody would give that benefit of the doubt to a webinar.

You're asking for trouble when you attempt to do your webinar on the fly with little rehearsal and without some form of a structure. At the very least, you need to follow an outline to make sure you deliver everything you promised in the allotted amount of time.

Building an outline

The roadmap to a successful presentation begins with an idea and grows from there. List a series of topics that work well for a discussion. That provides the framework for your storyboard or outline (they're basically the same thing and are used interchangeably) as you continue to prioritize each idea. An *outline* is basically a list of things you plan to do and say in some order. It acts as a diagram for your script and itinerary, but it takes some time to hone. After some group brainstorming — or pretty serious thought if you're doing it on your own — you can elaborate the themes and come up with the best strategy to present them.

Here are some tips for writing your outline:

- **Determine the goal for your webinar:** Ask yourself what you hope the audience gets out of your webinar. And what do *you* want to accomplish? Anything contrary to that goal should be nixed.
- **List your ideas:** By identifying the main categories of your discussion, you can strategize problems, arguments, and solutions. Afterward, you can put them in linear form (the order in which you are going to present them).
- **Pick your team:** It's not quite the same as picking sides for kickball at recess, but then again, it's not totally different. After you decide how you want to approach the subject matter, you can determine which speakers will work best for the theme.

TIP

- **Consider the proper format:** Some webinars works well with a single speaker, whereas others are more suited for multiple voices. If one person can deliver the message, stick with that format. However, if you wish to show variations to the theme, go with several other experts.
- **Supporting slides:** What kind of visual aids will work best to get your message across? Remember, the slides act as the appetizer, but they are not the main course. They're there to support your overall message.

Writing a title slide

TIP

Motivation comes in many forms, so one way to get focused and stay that way involves making a slide with the name of the presentation, as seen in Figure 5-1. Just keep it at one until you have a concrete theme. The biggest problem with some producers is that they make slides early in the process and sometimes they aren't consistent with the final content. It's best to work from an outline and build a story from it before finalizing your slides. Look at your webinar as a cohesive story you're trying to tell and make sure it's not just as a collection of information.

Figure 5-1: It doesn't have to be pretty, but putting the name of your presentation on a single slide just might stimulate your thought process.

Choosing content that matters

REMEMBER

First and foremost, a good presentation educates and helps its audience know a little bit more than before they logged on. That's a hefty responsibility, so make sure that your content supports the presentation, and isn't just eye (or mind) candy.

Here are some tips to consider:

- **It's up to you to convey the message:** The slides and other visual assets are there to help you tell the story. What you put on the slide should only be there to support your premise.
- **Make them look good:** Understanding the supporting role of PowerPoint slides provides a starting point, but making each one look spectacular helps dazzle the audience. Concentrate on a consistent design to further draw in your audience.
- **Go easy on the type:** I can't emphasize this enough: Don't go overboard on text. Every second your audience spends reading the slide is a second their attention isn't on what you're saying.
- **Pictures are worth a lot:** An image goes a long way when it comes to making a point. Just be sure to follow the rules I mention in Chapter 6.
- **Sometimes video is worth more:** In the YouTube-heavy world, the moving image plays a major role in providing maximum information. The more focused the video's message, as seen in Figure 5-2, the more effective it will be for your audience.
- **Talk the talk:** The presentation is like a discussion, first and foremost, so it's the presenter's show. She must always fill in the gaps with facts, anecdotes, and analogies, instead of just relying on the visuals. There are exceptions, but a general rule is to talk to the audience.

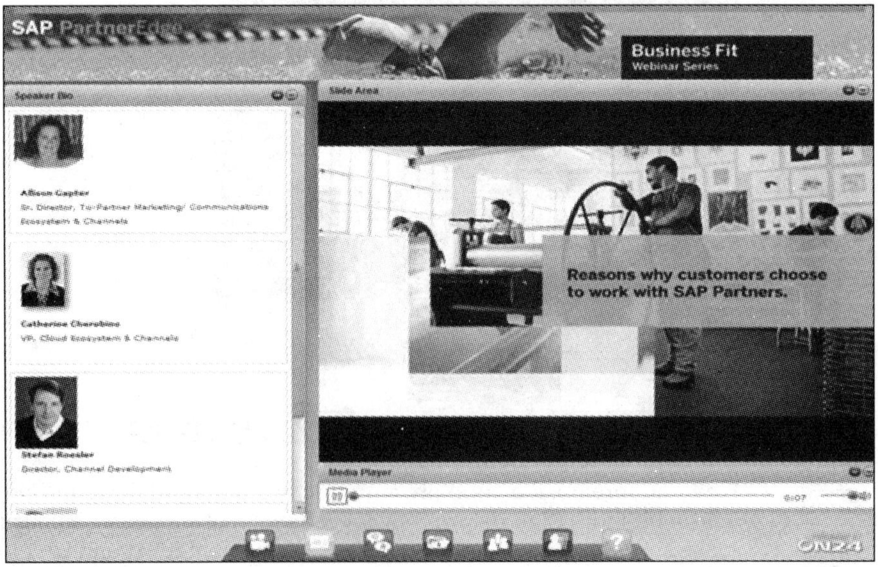

Figure 5-2: Video plays an important role in this SAP webinar run by ON24.

Identifying main points

REMEMBER

Think of the presenter as a tour guide at the Statue of Liberty taking the audience on a journey to the island and up to the great lady. You explain what you're going to tell attendees throughout the course of the session and how the presentation will flow.

You can do the following:

- **Provide basic operational info:** Explain the housekeeping aspects of the session so the audience knows how everything works.
- **Dissect the session:** Break down the presentation to your participants and emphasize each major part of the webinar by providing an overview of each individual topic.
- **Go deeper with reasoning:** Try to list five reasons that make your point for the discussion and then go through them one by one. By identifying these main points, you show the audience the structure in the beginning and you summarize your presentation in the end. But first it needs to be apparent to you. When it's done correctly, the audience knows what they can expect and will stick around to hear it play out.

Evaluating the level of detail

How much detail is enough? Different presentations require different levels of detail, so there's no hard-and-fast rule. That amount of detail depends on the type of story that you're telling. For example, if you're giving a thought leadership presentation on a high-level concept, obviously you don't need to be overly detailed.

TIP

On the other hand, if you're giving a demo of a specific product, you may need more detail that can help the participant understand the product, its features, and what it can do for them. A good rule is to consider that details should only be added when it supports the story. Remember, it's all about the speaker informing and/or convincing the audience.

Comparing your content to your end goal

When evaluating your message, it's important to take into consideration all the different parts of the webinar and how they complement one another leading up to the answers you're trying to provide. If you're feeling it doesn't work in rehearsal or even before that, it's time to reevaluate.

Although this evaluation process is rather complex, here are a few areas to consider:

- **Outline:** Be sure that your webinar has the proper balance between topics and assets (slides, demonstrations, movies, and so on). Also make sure there's adequate time for each.
- **Script:** Is it snappy and interesting, or does it drone on? Even if you use a script for just the opening and closing remarks, it must compel the participant to want to stay online.
- **Format:** Decide if the format works for the subject matter. For example, will a single speaker thoroughly cover the topic? Or is it best to have multiple speakers, or turn it into an interview-style format? Multiple perspectives or controversial topics do well with a moderated panel.
- **Presenters:** Make sure that each presenter effectively adds to the conversation, has appeal, and is never redundant.
- **Interactivity:** Be sure that there's a nice mix of interactivity throughout the session, including polls, Q&A, and chat (when applicable). This keeps the audience engaged.

Creating an Effective Flow

REMEMBER

Like a mighty river, as seen in Figure 5-3, your webinar needs a really strong flow. That begins with an effective storyboard or outline (they're interchangeable at that point) and the right balance of speakers, content, and interactivity.

A nicely flowing webinar depends heavily on effective structure, preparation, and rehearsal. It has a very distinct narrative that always reminds people of where they are in the presentation. But it's not a one-off deal. Great webinar flow isn't just within one presentation. If you have multiple presentations, not only should each of them flow on their own, but they should flow together as a cohesive piece, throughout all of the different pieces you have in your presentation.

You should consider not only your story, but also the use of interactive tools, how you're managing different speakers, and how you're managing the Q&A. A webinar has a lot of different moving parts and you need to consider them all when you're trying to make sure you have a good, consistent flow.

Consider the following:

- **Do effective housekeeping:** Basically, this refers to the presenter's opening remarks telling the audience what to expect and explaining all of the technical parts of the webinar.

- **Poll your attendees:** After each section, you should live-poll the audience to make sure you have your finger on its pulse and also as a way to break up a presentation and create a natural flow. This can also provide useful market insights, in real time.
- **Stick to the schedule:** Remember all the things that are taking place in the webinar, from production and housekeeping, to your actual presentation, to your speaker's schedule, and the Q&A.

Figure 5-3: A flowing river moves downstream.

Interactivity

REMEMBER

Like recess or gym class, participation from everyone (presenter to participant) is a big part of the webinar process, so there's not one set of rules when it comes to interacting with your guests. The value of interactivity is that you want to have a real conversation with your audience. Remember, you don't want to talk at them; you want to have a meaningful discussion with them.

These days you have quite an array of tools at your disposal to allow you to interact in various ways. Think of each as using the proper club when playing golf. Each situation on the course has its own unique solution, just like your presentation. Like golf clubs, interactive tools can serve your presentations in a lot of different ways. You need to pick the interactive tool that works best for the type of conversation you want to have with your audience. Before getting into the different value with each type, take a look at the three basic kinds of interactive conversations:

- **Presenter to audience:** Basically, it's a talking head seen by the audience on their screen, as seen in Figure 5-4.
- **Audience to presenter:** Whether it's responding to a poll or asking a question during the Q&A portion of the presentation, the participant plays an active role in the live webinar.
- **Audience to audience:** Your participants can communicate with one another through social media during the presentation using Twitter and Facebook, for example. The group chat widget facilitates communication within the environment, too.

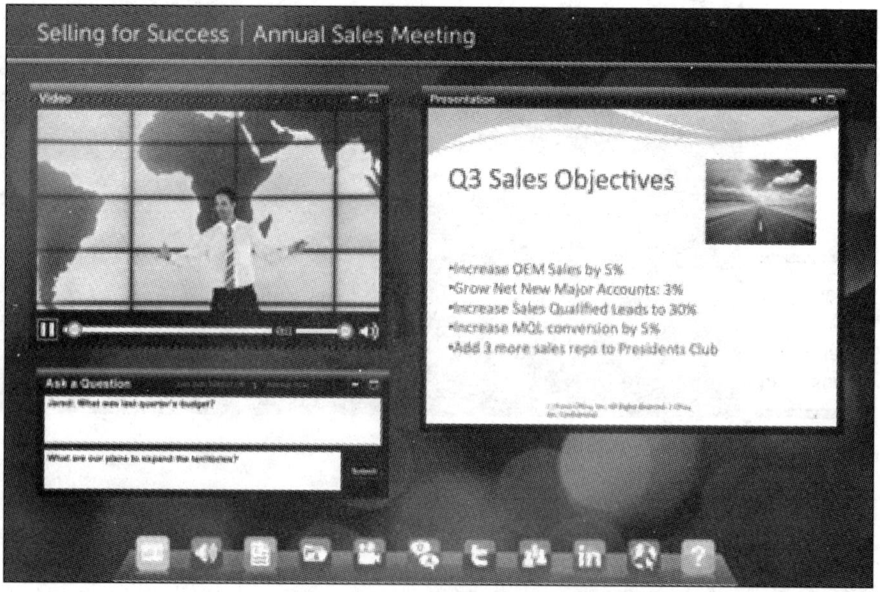

Figure 5-4: The presenter occupies some real estate on the screen during this annual sales presentation.

Here's a rundown of some webinar interaction tools. They all have different benefits, so pick the ones that are right for your needs.

Chat

WARNING!

Chat is a way of creating a secondary dialogue for conversation within the webinar experience by allowing participants to communicate amongst each other. Some producers have mixed feelings about it, however. It's something you'll have to experiment with to decide whether it's right for you. Part of the reason some producers don't like it is that it creates a separate conversation during the presentation. Depending on the type of discussion you're having, that can be good or bad. The positive side is that it encourages dialogue and participation. It's a good idea to have one or two people monitoring the chat to maintain order and answer questions. The downside of chat is that you can get negative comments, which can be a distraction.

Polls and surveys

TIP

Polling is a nice way to bring the audience's voice into the presentation. You get to hear the voice of the audience and bring it into the discussion, and they get to do the same. Most audience members have a natural curiosity about what their peers are thinking and doing. By seeing the results of polls, they can find similarities or differences with others. "What's someone else doing? Am I the same?" That's a big part of what's on an audience member's mind during a presentation.

Q&A

TIP

The Q&A is the most interactive tool in the webinar experience, and it's probably used in about 85 percent of webinars. (Who knows how much longer the other 15 percent who don't use it can survive?) Typically, it's done at the end of the presentation, but an increasing number of webinars integrate Q&A throughout the presentation, as seen in Figure 5-5. The expanded use of Q&A can be effective at creating a real conversation, but the downside is that it slows down the presentation.

That's why you must allot enough time to adequately answer as many questions as possible. If you promise a question-and-answer period in a one-hour webinar, but your presentation lasts for 58 minutes and you only allow two minutes for your Q&A, you've reneged on the promise of having a discussion with the audience. You want to make sure you deliver your presentation on time, so depending on your structure, plan for it accordingly.

TIP

If the time allotted doesn't allow you to answer all the questions asked, develop a Q&A document with unanswered questions and then provide that to attendees.

Figure 5-5: A Q&A graphic.

Social media integration

The magic of social media has increasingly become an effective tool for webinars today, as seen in Figure 5-6, because it continues the discussion by broadcasting the conversation beyond the console and beyond the webinar participant to an extended audience. If someone is impressed with your content and they tweet about it, it goes out to an extended network. Of course, the downside is that they're not always pleased, and they let others know about that, too. You can read more about webinars and social media in Chapter 9.

Figure 5-6: Social media is an important tool in the virtual trainer's toolbox.

Developing Different Outline Styles for Different Webinars

In the kitchen, sometimes I follow a recipe to the letter. Other times, I go completely on a whim, and often I do something in the middle. The same holds true for a webinar. Although planning and scripting are a big part of the process for a successful presentation, some webinars are easier to outline than others. In addition, different formats require different degrees of preparation.

Single speaker

Think of your speaker as the host of the show. Sometimes she introduces a guest; other times, it's a solo effort. The host often administers the Q&A, either answering the questions or feeding questions to appropriate guest. An outline for a single-speaker event should include opening and closing remarks.

Interview-style

REMEMBER

Turn your webinar into your own talk show with this format. The main presenter channels their inner Anderson Cooper and provides information through one-on-one interviews as opposed to a lengthy discussion. When you're in a straight interview format, video becomes so much more important, especially when it comes to setting up each guest. Seeing the presenter and guests helps the attendee observe body language and facial expressions in addition to talking. This goes a long way when it comes to making the attendee feel comfortable with what's being said.

Here are some of the aspects you should consider:

- **Identify the format:** Make sure your potential audience knows the format of the presentation before they register. That way, they know what to expect.
- **Interview questions:** Besides scripting the opening remarks, create a list of questions to ask your guests.
- **Time management:** The lack of scripting and the unpredictability of each answer make it hard to know exactly how long each interview will run. Brief each guest beforehand on the questions and ask them to keep their answers brief when possible.
- **Host remarks:** In your opening remarks, be sure to identify each guest and their area of expertise. Your closing remarks should alert your audience where to find more information on the topic. Often additional resources are available for download in the webinar console itself.

Moderated panel

Having a panel of guests for your presentation shares many similarities with the interview format, with the exception that the guests are all talking at once. That makes you more like a referee than a host. You have to ask the questions and make sure the event stays on time. In addition, you'll have the bigger challenge of making sure that everyone plays nice together and doesn't talk over one another.

Instead of building a presentation, you could prepare a set of questions or topics that would be discussed to the panel. The topics are pre-conceived, so that each of the panel members gets a chance to review the content and to prepare some comments. Sometimes you create supporting slides in advance. The storyboard — the narrative, the outline — is not a presentation. Instead, it's based on a set of topics or questions. Those questions, typically, should appear on the screen. You have the choice of having an open-ended conversation with not much to look at, or creating some supporting slides based on each topic to create visual support for the discussion that takes place.

Interactive

Most webinars already have some level of interactivity, so it's misleading to call interactivity a format unto itself. Some webinars obviously have more interactive elements than others, like the amount of polling, the presence of a Q&A, or the use of social media. Interactivity should be present in all presentations in one form or another.

Going from Outline to Script

Every presentation begins with some form of outline, or at least, the logic behind putting it all together. Whether it's thoroughly structured on paper, or lives partially in your head, an outline is the essence of your presentation. The more you outline your presentation, the more you storyboard, and the more you figure out the flow, the more effective it tends to be.

Deciding whether you need a formal script

Nobody would confuse a webinar script with a screenplay for a movie, but that doesn't make it any less important. A good script is the cornerstone of a great movie, and an equally impressive presentation, but a webinar script is not meant to be read from start to finish. That would be too robotic and dry. When the webinar is pre-recorded, it's even more important that the content be presented in a way that suggests a live broadcast. Audiences prefer the "feel" of a live webinar; it just seems more authentic. Instead, the script is more of a set of guidelines rather then something meant to be read word-for-word.

Remember the following:

- **Include the basics:** Typically the script includes the introduction, the housekeeping (letting the attendee know the lay of the land before getting started), and perhaps the first slide or two to get things going.
- **Less is more:** Effective webinars are great conversations, and great conversations happen when people are just shooting the breeze. Reading fully scripted material generally doesn't evoke that message, and instead sounds a bit staged.
- **Speakers differ:** Every presenter is a little different. Some are not comfortable speaking extemporaneously about the topic. For that situation, it's acceptable to use a script. Just adjust it accordingly to fit the speaker.

Going live without an outline, script, or net

It's critical to use a script when you're not as familiar with your subject matter, or when you've got a very specific message that you are trying to stay on script with. It's also a good idea when the presenters are simply not comfortable in the medium. Ninety-five percent of presenters don't use scripts, however.

Turning bullet points into words

Limit the number of bullets on a page and limit the amount of text that follows each bullet.

Managing Time

A webinar is not like a Bruce Springsteen concert that can run for hours without a predictable end and nobody minds. You have no such luxury with a webinar, nor do participants clamor for it. When it comes to time management, nothing is more important than respecting your audience. If you plan on delivering a 60-minute webinar, you're making a commitment that you're going to deliver what you promised.

Consider the following:

- **Don't run late:** Never go over your allotted time. Even if it's a great webinar with a lot of interactivity and you just want to keep going, don't. Your audience members may have prior commitments or other stuff to do. You're forcing them into making a decision that they don't want to have to make. You made an agreement to start and end at a specific time. Make sure you stick to it.
- **Have a leisurely start time:** It's become an acceptable norm to start slowly to give participants time to move from one meeting to the next, but that doesn't mean you shouldn't go live at your start time. It's not about starting late, but more like starting off with a long hello to give people time to get settled in before you get to the good stuff.
- **Take a few minutes to explain the basics:** Tell the audience what to expect for the presentation and explain the technology to them. If there are interactive tools, they need to be highlighted. Describe the Q&A area of the console and the integrated Twitter conversation.

Accurate scheduling

Viewing times are going up, and audiences are willing to stay for an hour. But audiences are savvy and can detect when you're delivering filler, so the golden rule is to create a webinar length that corresponds with length of content that you have to offer. If you've got 20 minutes of great content, advertise a 30-minute webinar. Do 20 minutes of content and a 10-minute Q&A. If you got 45 minutes of great content, do a one-hour webinar with a 15-minute Q&A. It's okay to end a little early, but it's not okay to end a little late.

A realistic agenda

When it comes to planning your presentation schedule, you need to account for all the different elements, not just the presentation. That includes the interactive elements, the housekeeping, the Q&A, and so on in terms of planning your time. To assure that it works, you need to rehearse it. In rehearsal, you'll learn where you are going to be in terms of length. It's important to remember to respect that amount of time to honor the contract that you are entering with your audience.

Speaker direction

Depending on the structure of your webinar, it's important for the speakers to understand their role. That's the job of the host, and it all begins in the planning stage.

Host a call in advance with all of your speakers to talk about ideas for the presentation. Then have another call to discuss the presentations themselves. You should also have a rehearsal call. You don't always have to have everyone give their full presentations in rehearsals, but rehearse the flow.

The host runs the calls and tells all the different speakers what's going to happen. For example, "I'm going to introduce everybody, do the housekeeping, and welcome everybody. Then I'm going to introduce the presentation and the flow of the webinar. Next I'm going to introduce Speaker A and then hand it to you. When you're done, you're going to hand it back to me. I'm going to say a few more words and do a poll, and then I'm going to ask you for your thoughts on that poll. When you're done, I'm going to introduce the next speaker."

It is the host's responsibility to make sure that everybody understands their role and where the handoffs are going to be between speakers. That includes understanding who is going be administering the Q&A. There are tools within some webinar consoles, as seen in Figure 5-7, that you can use to help alert people to where they are in the presentation. For instance, most webinar platforms allow for speaker chat where the speakers can chat with each other without the audience's knowledge. So you can say, "Hey, you're going a little long," or tell the next speaker to get ready because they're up in five minutes.

Figure 5-7: This ON24 webinar console allows for speaker chat.

Chapter 6

Making Your Point with PowerPoint

In This Chapter

- Understanding PowerPoint
- Unleashing the power of the slide
- Controlling the presentation
- Integrating pictures and graphics

Saying that PowerPoint helps you make a point with power is a cliché, because more importantly, it allows you to make your point with ease. Within a few moments of firing up the program, you can create a slide presentation to support your talking points and enhance it further with pictures, audio, and video. It's hard to imagine the days before it existed. (That time wasn't that long ago, in the era of big hair, New Wave music, and monochromatic computers that cost as much as a living room set.)

REMEMBER

The precursor to the webinar, the seminar, was usually held live in a crowded banquet room, and the visual part of the show came from photographic slides, replete with the clunky sound of a projector.

Although the presentation often had a quaint effectiveness, it was also inconvenient by today's standards because everyone was required to gather in the same location at the same time, increasing the budget for the company or individual.

Presentation quality was another factor because it was often tied to the budget. Back then, graphics were constructed by art departments, laid out under a camera specializing in photographing flat art, and captured on slide film. If there was a glitch (or change in statistics), you could do nothing but advance to the next slide.

And then there were the cruder methods. For some presentations, the host drew on a dry erase board; other times, it was a chalk board. (Hey, at least the squeaking of the chalk kept you alert.) Then there was the uninspiring technique of hand-drawing words and symbols on a giant flip chart. (You know, like a humongous pad that the Jolly Green Giant would use to write his grocery list.) These techniques made people think that seminars were boring and uncool.

Microsoft changed the presentation game in 1990 with the introduction of PowerPoint. Suddenly, the user could easily create sophisticated slides on the fly and present them on-screen. That benefit changed the complexity of meetings, classroom lectures, and the predecessor to the webinar, the seminar.

In this chapter, I show you how PowerPoint can help enhance the delivery of your webinar.

Understanding the Effectiveness of Graphics

If a picture is worth a thousand words, how much does its value increase when you add a phrase to go with it? Mixing words and pictures has long been an effective way to communicate an idea. Think about that for a second. Would you rather spend three-and-a-half minutes describing how a little kitten got stuck hanging on a tree branch and never gave up, or instead show an image that gets the point across in a single glance? Add text like *Hang in there, baby*, and you not only have an effective statement for a meme, but also the formula to one of the bestselling posters of the 1970s.

Memes

Memes by definition are ideas and behaviors that spread through culture, but these days they often take on the quality of an inside joke. Visual memes are virally transmitted symbols over the web that often include pictures with ironic text that cover a variety of themes, from political to humorous to social commentary. If you have a Facebook account, chances are you've seen one. They are the pictures with the sometimes humorous, other times offensive words that some people post. The term was coined in 1976 by British evolutionary biologist Richard Dawkins in *The Selfish Gene* to discuss the evolutionary principles in explaining the spread of ideas and cultural phenomena.

What was true back in the era of bell bottoms and bubble type remains true today, minus, of course, the bell bottoms and bubble type. The combination of graphics and a phrase clearly helps get your point across and keep the audience engaged. That's because people get bored listening to a talking head yammer on without some form of visual stimulation to go with it. That's why it's so important to use graphics to support your discussion. But don't think that any image will do. It all harkens back to the old *garbage in, garbage out* theory.

Reaping the benefits of how screen graphics enhance your discussion begins with understanding how to use PowerPoint.

Discovering PowerPoint Essentials

It wasn't that long ago when a public speaking engagement required a slide projector — if you were lucky — to display the session's visual assets. PowerPoint brought that idea into the modern age by allowing the presenter to also be the slide maker. You supply the content – clever writing, graphics, video, and so on — and PowerPoint does the rest.

PowerPoint lets you easily create a presentation by building individual slides, altering the order to fit your speech, and saving it in a format that looks good on a projection screen or the output device for your participant. But just because it's easy doesn't mean that you should breeze through putting your slides together. The effectiveness of your slides depends heavily on proper design and uniformity.

A slide show helps convey a story through a series of projected images. In the photography world, that meant taking a picture of an object or carefully laid-out words and pictures. It was tedious and time-consuming. PowerPoint makes it easy. By letting you create a presentation and customize each slide to fit your needs in terms of content, the limits are nonexistent.

Know the lay of the land

PowerPoint is both simple and complex to use. More appropriately, it's simple when you understand how it works — at least when you know where to find the necessary tools — and complicated when you're constantly searching for them. After you know how it's arranged, you can make a slide rather quickly. How quick? Well, that depends on the content and layout. Figure 6-1 shows the basic layout of the program.

Figure 6-1: The full PowerPoint layout.

Here's an overview of the program:

- **Menu bar:** This is the area at the top of the screen where all menus are displayed.
- **Standard toolbar:** The standard toolbar displays the name of the presentation (in this case, *Webinars For Dummies*) and buttons for common tasks, such as opening, saving, and printing a presentation.
- **Ribbon:** This tabbed command bar at the top of a window or work area organizes features into logical groups. The Home tab and Themes tab have the most commonly used commands for formatting presentation content and design.
- **Thumbnails in left pane:** Each represents the different slides you were working on.
- **Slide:** Click a slide in the Thumbnails pane and to display a full version.
- **Placeholders:** This is the area on the slide for adding content. The slide layout determines which placeholders appear on a slide.
- **Notes pane:** The Notes pane is the section for the user to type reference notes for the presentation. Only the presenter can see it.

Familiarity between versions

Depending on the version of PowerPoint you're running, things on your machine may look a little different than the figures in this book. No worries. Most of the functions and features discussed here have changed little, if at all, over the last few versions.

Change the view

If you want to alter the look and feel of the workspace, you have the choice of three views. Just click the bottom left to shift between each one.

At the bottom left, as seen in the following figure, you have three views:

- **Normal:** Normal is the standard view that shows the slide sorter and the selected slide.
- **Slide Sorter:** Slide Sorter shows the individual slides. This mode is great for moving and arranging slides in their proper order.
- **Slide Show:** Slide Show view plays your slides as a self-playing show.

Make your slides

Chess, carpentry, and playing the piano may be fairly easy to learn, yet each can take a lifetime to master. PowerPoint, too, falls in that category, almost. Even if you've never touched the software, after a quick primer and a few step-by-step instructions, you'll be able to create your first slide, another, and after that, a more ambitious one. Before long, you'll have a presentation ready to, well, present.

These individual slides can include keywords, pictures, video, and audio too. On the program side, PowerPoint provides more than one way to create your presentation, but it all begins with the basics.

After you fire up PowerPoint, you want to create a new presentation. (That is, unless you already created one. In that case, you can work on an existing saved one, or work from one of the built-in templates.) Begin with the basic presentation:

1. **Go to File⇨New Presentation, as seen in Figure 6-2.**

   In the workspace, you'll notice that the first slide is there. One slide does not make a show, so you will want to create several.

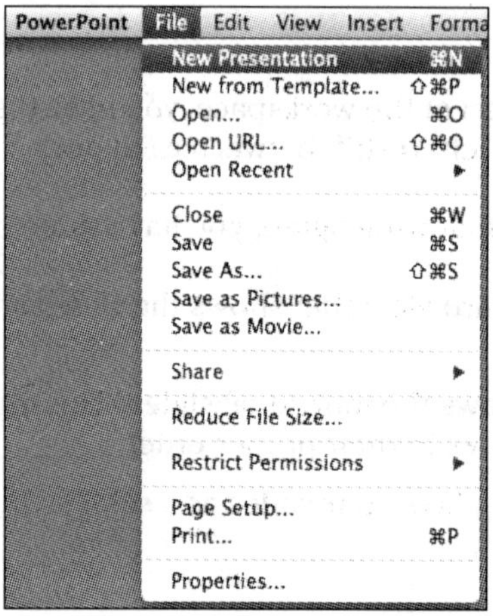

Figure 6-2: Creating a new presentation is as easy as going to the File menu.

2. **Click the Home tab and select New Slide one time for each additional slide you need.**

   If you click the New Slide button, as seen in the following figure on the right side of the layout, you will see numerous choices in the dialog.

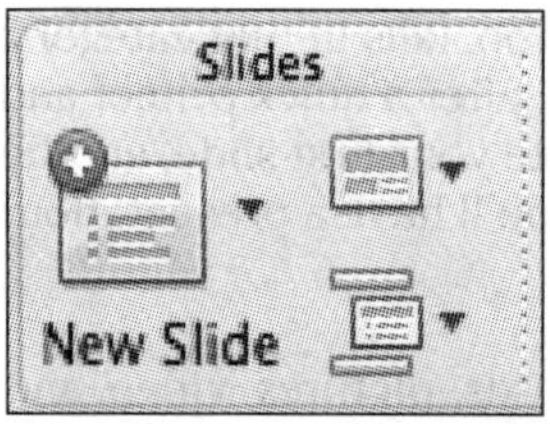

3. **When you create a slide, it's blank, as seen in Figure 6-3. To fill it out with pertinent information, click the placeholder and either type on it or click to search for other content.**

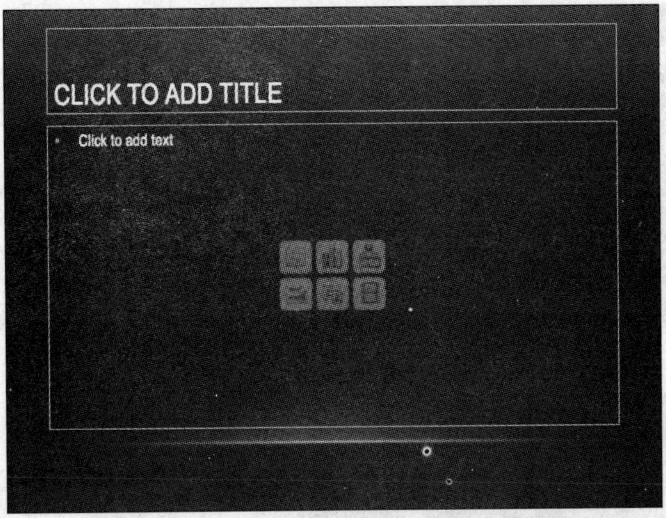

Figure 6-3: When you create a slide, it's blank.

4. **Add content.**

   Depending on the type of slide you choose, you can add content other than text. The content slide provides buttons, as seen in Figure 6-4, that allow you to insert the following: Table, Chart, Smart Art Graphic, Picture, Clip Art, or Movie. Besides clicking the button to navigate to your content, you can also drag and drop or copy and paste into the placeholder.

Figure 6-4: Content slides have buttons that allow you to easily import various types of content.

5. **Resize the placeholder to make sure pictures and text are the proper size.**

   After changing the text size to 60 points, as shown in Figure 6-5, you'll notice it's justified to the left. It's easy to center it. Just grab the anchors until a four-arrowed move icon appears and push or pull to get the size or placement just right, as shown in Figure 6-6.

Figure 6-5: Text for this placeholder is justified to the left.

Figure 6-6: Moving a placeholder is as simple as grabbing the anchors and moving them in or out.

6. **You can apply a theme and a layout for all of your slides instead of setting them individually for each slide.**

   A *theme* defines the presentation fonts, colors, backgrounds, and effects. *Layout* defines how content is arranged on a slide.

7. **Format your slide content.**

   You can adjust the size of each placeholder as well as the size of the content inside it. Move the pointer over the border of the title placeholder, and when the cursor appears as a four-headed arrow, click the border. The blue border and sizing handles indicate that the entire placeholder is selected.

8. **When you're satisfied with your presentation, go to File⇨Save As, navigate to the desired folder (create one in the dialog box if you have not already), name the presentation, and save it.**

Decide on a layout

PowerPoint provides templates for different slide layout types. These define how content appears on each slide in your presentation. Basically each choice provides a variation in the position, number, and type of placeholders. Some are great for text slides, whereas others let you add a variety of visual information. If you click the arrow on the right side of the New Slide button, you'll see a variety of options for slide themes and formats, as seen in Figure 6-7. These include

- **Title:** Use it at the beginning of your presentation. Provides two placeholders, one for the title and the other for the subtitle.
- **Title and Content:** The most commonly used slide layout works pretty well. The top placeholder supports your heading, and the larger one below it can be used for any other content you deem appropriate, including pictures, video, or a chart. This layout also handles a bullet list quite well.
- **Section Header:** It's like a double-title slide. Use to illustrate different sections of the presentation, as opposed to two separate title slides.
- **Two Content:** Lets you import two different types of content that sit side by side.
- **Comparison:** Similar to the Two Content layout but with a placeholder to add text above it. This one's great for showing differences in photos, charts, or other information graphics.
- **Title Only:** Pretty self-explanatory. Use this one for a title. By default, its placeholder sits on the top of the page. You can still insert other content by copying and pasting or going through the Insert menu.
- **Blank:** This slide has no placeholder, but you can still add content by either copying and pasting or going to Insert⇨Photo. It works well when showing images on their own. You can adjust the size of an image by dragging anchors.
- **Content with Caption:** Places the content on the right side of the slide and the caption on the left. This theme works well when designing a chart or information graphic.
- **Picture with Caption:** Position the picture on the slide with its caption below it.
- **Title and Vertical Text:** Mixes normal (horizontal) text with vertical text.
- **Vertical Title and Text:** Use both placeholders for vertical text.

Many companies use a slide template to ensure branding consistency.

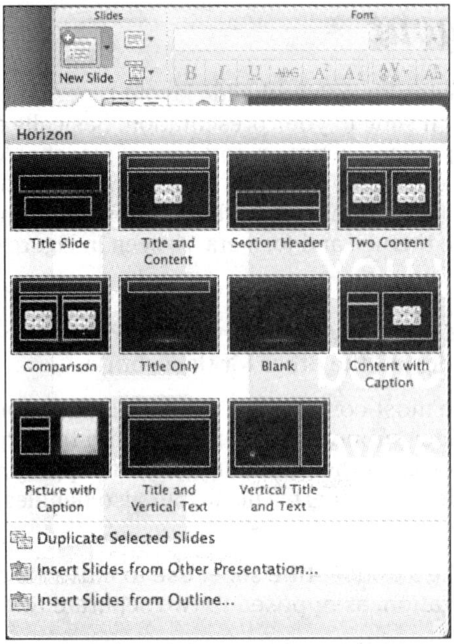

Figure 6-7: A variety of options for your new slide.

Take advantage of speaker notes

TIP

Sometimes the speaker needs a reminder of what the slide represents, so PowerPoint lets you add reference notes for each one, as seen in Figure 6-8. These small writings help the speaker emphasize the main points of the discussion. Although you as the presenter can see it on the computer screen on the podium or in front of you, it remains hidden from the viewer. While you're putting the presentation together, you can add whatever notes you deem applicable. You can also print these notes — along with a thumbnail version of the appropriate slide — as a reference to use when making the presentation.

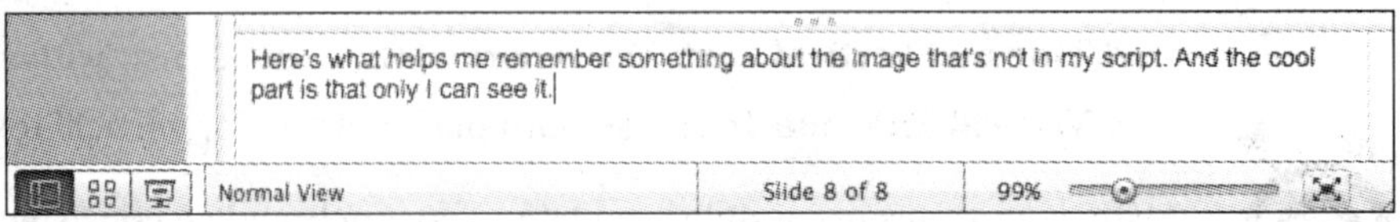

Figure 6-8: The Speaker Notes section helps you to know exactly what the slide represents, just in case it's not in your script.

Use a remote

If you're close to your keyboard, you can manually advance each slide using the up and down arrow keys. But then again, just because you can, doesn't mean you should. Most of the time, you're better off using a dedicated remote control so that you don't mess things up by hitting the wrong key or command during the webinar.

Not that long ago, basic remote control models connected to the USB connector on your computer, although you'd be hard-pressed to find a tethered one these days because wireless models are so inexpensive and ubiquitous.

TIP

But that's not the only solution. For example, Macintosh users can also use their remote control. Or you could download an app for iPhone or Android that turns your smartphone into a remote control.

Here are your choices:

- **Dedicated remote control:** Wireless and inexpensive, these USB-powered remote controls not only advance your slides but also include other presentation tools. For example, many models include a laser pointer.
- **Apple remote:** If you own a Macintosh computer and have the remote that comes with it, as seen in Figure 6-9, you can use it in a pinch to control the presentation. It will work within 30 feet of your computer, which is about 28 feet more than you'll need.
- **Smartphone:** Download an app that transforms your Android device or Apple iPhone into a remote control. There are many apps to choose from, so make certain that the one you pick includes what you need.

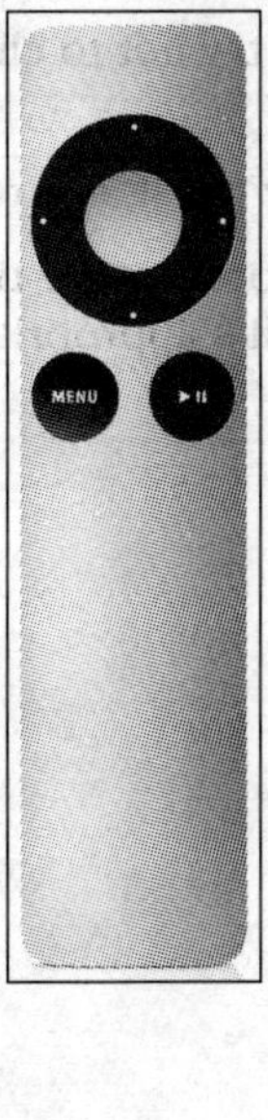

Figure 6-9: An Apple remote control.

Composing Slides

It doesn't take a university study to realize that an audience can develop an attention deficit when the only source of information is a talking head. But a boring or informative slide doesn't help much either. If you think the way to supplement a boring discussion is to pack a bunch of words on a slide, or use a font that's not immediately readable, you will still lose your audience despite having visual aids.

REMEMBER

Holding the audience's attention is a battle fought on many fronts. To grab their attention for a presentation, you should adhere to time-honored techniques. It all begins with figuring out your overall message and how you can break that message down into individual points. At the same time, you need to make sure that it's easily understood. Remember, a full multimedia experience is more than slamming words and pictures together.

Keep design simple and consistent

Using graphics to accompany a discussion doesn't exactly break new ground. Chances are that our prehistoric ancestors used cave drawings as a visual aid for a discussion on the *meat-good, hunger-bad* theme. Visual references simply engage the audience's attention and help them further understand the topic. Acknowledging the need for visual accompaniment is one thing, but creating an effective one is quite another. The key is that each visual message remains neat, clean, and consistent, and that the presenter doesn't get more dependent on the technology than the message.

Consider the following:

TIP

- **Keep it simple:** Use one slide for each topic, and try not to change slides more than twice per minute.
- **Be efficient:** Only use slides that emphasize your point, not repeat it.
- **Use images:** Sometimes they represent a lot of words; other times, they're enhanced by a few more. Just make sure it's appropriate, as seen in Figure 6-10.

Figure 6-10: Using the blossoming cotton boll as a comparison effectively makes an analogy that works with a variety of points.

And here's what to avoid:

- **Too much text on a slide:** You add text to summarize a point, not to make the audience read long-winded text.
- **Predictable clip art:** Think "predictable clip art" is redundant? Perhaps, but sometimes you have to use clip art. When you do, do so sparingly, and then only when you don't have a suitable replacement. Sometimes, it's a cliché, as shown in Figure 6-11.
- **Illegible fonts:** What you may think is a cool font can actually be unreadable to your audience. Stick to clean, evenly spaced fonts.
- **Try to avoid (too many) bullets:** Conserve your bullets. Although they're great for getting to the point, overusing them deflates their value.
- **Maintain your focus:** Remember, your PowerPoint slides help strengthen your point, not the reverse. Don't let your message take a back seat to your PowerPoint slides. Stick to the main points of discussion and let PowerPoint support supplementary information.

Figure 6-11: A boring clip art image of a phone used for a conference call. Unless it's for the conference call museum, it's not effective.

Write your own text

WARNING!

Face it: The task of finding suitable content for your slides is a drag sometimes, and copying and pasting it into PowerPoint makes life easier, but it also can set you down the path for trouble. Although it simplifies the process, in many ways, it's a bad practice. Not only can it put you on the edge of plagiarism, but someone else's recycled words can be dramatically different than the ones that would come out of your mouth.

On a procedural level, it also introduces style variations with font types and sizes that don't match the rest of your slides. This can make the whole set look like a hodgepodge. Sure, you can fix it, but if you need to adjust each one anyway, why bother? Originality remains king, so be careful when you see an idea that you would like to use in one of your slides. Instead, put all ideas in your own words.

Consider the following:

TIP

- **Use Word (or another word processing program):** If you don't want to type directly on the slide, you can type and edit your content in a Word document. This allows you to work with the content and desired style, and then copy and paste the content you've created into PowerPoint when you're happy with it.
- **Acknowledge the source:** If you use someone else's material, always credit them either on the slide or verbally.

Give your slides a visual theme

Sometimes people take the uniformity of their presentation for granted. You wouldn't go to work wearing brown striped pants, black shoes, and a blue polka dot shirt. If you did, your matching skills would certainly raise eyebrows. The same applies when it comes to your slides. They too should coordinate. That doesn't mean they should all look the same, but they should at the very least share a common theme.

Consider the following:

- **Continuity:** You should strive for consistency when it comes to the look and feel of each slide. Style, placement, and size should work together.
- **Color:** Use bold color for emphasis with either muted or colorless (pale, white, grayscale, black) text for support.
- **Fonts:** Don't mix typefaces. It confuses the viewer. That means if you choose Helvetica, don't all of a sudden switch to another font like Impact or Times New Roman. Also, use a consistent font size: for example, 30-point for titles, 24-point for keywords, and 20-point for bullet lists. (If you're already using a corporate template, that takes care of consistency for you.)
- **Letter case:** If you want to be edgy and use all lowercase characters, that's your choice, but be consistent.
- **Style:** Once again, the key here is consistency. If you plan to present titled items in italics, don't mistakenly use quotation marks for some of them. If you plan to use all caps for keywords, don't use capitalization for other words.

Prioritize keywords over sentences

Not only do keywords economize your thoughts and ideas, but they also increase readability of the slides. That can go a long way when it comes to the overall webinar. If the audience is taking a long time reading the slides, they're probably not paying full attention to you. Keywords get the point across quickly. Phrases like "Quota met" or "Sales increased by half" get right to the point. Use them instead of long, drawn-out wording. You can emphasize keywords using a variety of techniques. These include

- **Highlight on-screen:** You can easily create this effect in PowerPoint and simply highlight the keywords, much as you would with a highlighter on paper.
- **Use annotations:** PowerPoint lets you uses arrows, spotlights, and other effects to emphasize a keyword or phrase.
- **Change color:** You can use color to point out a keyword.

Bullet your points

Whether you're shooting skeet or emphasizing some interesting factoid in your presentation, you don't want to use too many bullets to get the job done. Overusing bullets in target shooting gets expensive, but overusing bullet points in your presentation lessens the impact of your statement. That's because the bullet is a bittersweet device. Its stock is high when used effectively, yet it plummets when overused. Bullet lists are quite helpful, but in the midst of a multimedia presentation, you need to rein them in in order to provide maximum impact.

A good practice for conserving bullets is to emphasize each point individually on a single slide, and then summarize at the end with a full bullet list. This allows each point to both stand on its own and be part of a collective.

Using Images

Viewers make a strong connection to pictures because they can communicate more effectively than a collection of words. That is why you want to use images sparingly to maximize their effect.

Here are some examples of good uses of images:

- **Context:** Using a single image or composite, you can show the relationship between two or more things.
- **Example:** Give a visual example that relates to the topic you're talking about.
- **Comparison:** Comparisons highlight the differences or changes to something, like before and after — for example, a freshly built snowman on one side, and a puddle with a hat, two pieces of coal, and a carrot on the other.
- **Analogy:** Great for explaining abstract ideas. Basically using an image to tell the audience, "This is what I mean." An example includes a set of images that shows an ambitious, hard worker at their desk, and another sipping a drinking in the pool in the yard of their mansion.
- **Demonstration:** By using several photos in succession, you can gradually take the viewers through a process, from beginning to end.
- **Visual cues:** Use images to let the viewer know what's next. Whether it's the next topic, speaker, or section, you can use a photo to get the point across.
- **Decoration:** Sometimes it's nice to use a great image just because it's pretty.

Add a photo to a slide

It's pretty easy to do. Just follow these easy steps:

1. **Create a new slide which you can add a picture to. Click the Picture icon on the placeholder or use the Insert Picture command on the toolbar, as seen in Figure 6-12. Locate the picture on your hard drive.**

   You can also opt to not insert a placeholder by choosing Insert and not selecting a placeholder.

2. **Click Insert.**

   The picture appears on the slide.

3. **After the picture appears on the slide, you can move or resize (if desired).**

Figure 6-12: The Insert Picture command on the toolbar provides another way to search for photos.

Make sure you have the photos on your computer

Before you can display images in your PowerPoint presentation, you need to get the pictures onto your computer.

There are several ways you can do it:

- **Scan from film or print:** Most likely, you will scan a piece of flat art, but you may have an older image shot on film that was never digitized.
- **Transfer from a digital camera, smartphone, or card:** Just plug your card reader in and grab the images you need.
- **Download from the web:** You can grab an image form a royalty-free image site, pay for one, or transfer one from a place that gave you permission.

Crop your picture in PowerPoint

REMEMBER

Don't worry about cropping your image before importing it on a PowerPoint slide. After you insert the photo, you will notice a little box, as shown in the following figure, that offers three choices.

These boxes (from left to right) do the following, and are self-explanatory:

- Manually repositions, resizes, or crops picture in the placeholder
- Crops picture in the placeholder
- Resizes picture to fit in the placeholder

Here's how to crop your picture:

1. **After selecting the image, click the first button.**

   It brings up the cropping box, as shown in Figure 6-13.

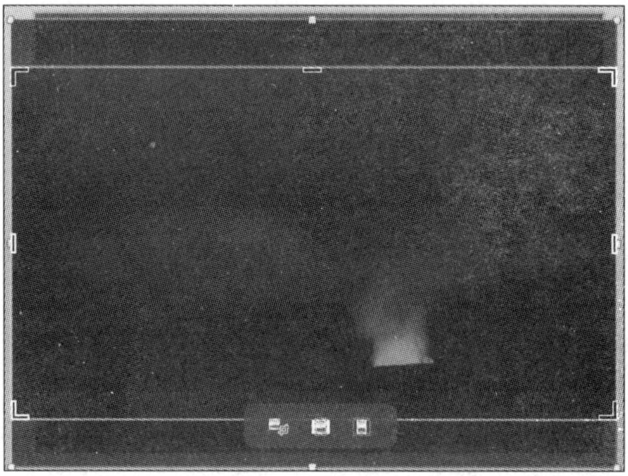

Figure 6-13: The cropping box.

2. **Push in the anchors (those markers on the corners). You can also move the picture by clicking in middle of the picture and holding the mouse button as you drag it to the desired position.**

   The final picture is shown in Figure 6-14.

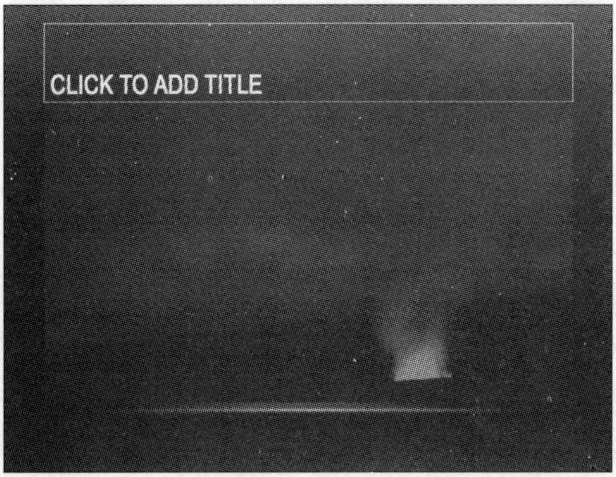

Figure 6-14: A cropped image.

Keep single pictures to each slide

Here's more of a suggestion than a rule: It's a good idea to keep your slides simple by using a single image to make your point. The exception to using multiple images happens when you're making a comparison, whether it show similarity or difference.

Show more photos than text slides

Images appeal to the visual senses, so it's probably a good idea to use less text on the slide when there's a picture on it too. Remember, chances are you're already providing a nice assortment of text, bullet lists, and keywords on other slides, so don't give photo slides more text than they need.

Use simple images

Your images should be clear and specific and not make the viewer scan them to figure out what point you're trying to make.

Avoid the following:

- Images with too much going on
- Out-of-focus pictures
- Badly composed images
- Pictures without a clear point of interest

Chapter 7

Establishing a Location

In This Chapter

- Find the best place for your webinar
- Setting up your webinar
- Considering great audio tips
- Connecting technology

Meeting in a physical space for a webinar is not much different than buying an audio CD to transfer music to your iPod. Yeah, you can do it, but it's not really necessary. It's no longer necessary to hold your next meeting in banquet hall or convention center to accommodate throngs of guests.

Think about it for a second. Filling a public space is nice for special occasions, but not warranted for every meeting. Who needs the additional responsibility of moving all the necessary gear from place to place? Wrangling stuff like projection units, podiums, and public address systems — not to mention having people at the door to check in registrants — is a lot of work. The virtual confines of your webinar provide the ideal location with none of the hassle.

Such logistical problems don't exist with a webinar because you can hold it anywhere as long as you have enough space to accommodate your speaker and the appropriate equipment. Anywhere from a lecture hall or an empty conference room to a television studio or a home office can work.

But how small is too small? Some trade shows have a webcasting service that conducts interviews in a makeshift booth that you can probably fit in your closet. Despite its gimmicky charm (and reliability), that's not the norm, however. The beauty of the webinar is that it's not important where you do it as long you have the proper means of connecting to the Internet and have something profound to tell people.

Events can happen in a variety of places, from sitting in your basement in front of an iPad to a soundstage with a multiple camera setup. More likely, however, you'll opt for your company's conference room, a speaker or two, and an effective PowerPoint presentation to spread the word.

Although your choice of webinar location is flexible, the main consideration is finding a location that has the right amount of space to carry out your plans. So although a single host in front of a webcam doesn't require much more than a walk-in closet in terms of a location, a television news-style event has much greater needs.

Selecting a Setting

REMEMBER

Whether you plan on shooting in the tightest space you can squeeze into or the most expansive room you can secure, it's all about finding the right spot. Remember, the audience is not physically in front of you — they're connected from all over the place via the Internet. So the area where you conduct the presentation only has to accommodate your needs. Theoretically, if you're doing a solo session, you could do it in your upstairs bathroom, providing it was well-lit and supported decent audio quality. (Not that I would recommend you host your next webinar from your bathroom, but it's possible.) On the other hand, if you're holding a moderated panel with several speakers using a multiple camera setup with a full technical support team, obviously your needs are a little more elaborate, costly, and take much longer to plan.

From a desktop

Webinars are clearly easier than organizing a meeting in a public space, but don't let that go to your head. Just because space is not a big concern doesn't mean you don't have other issues and concerns. For one, you have to have the proper equipment, and by proper equipment, I mean being up to the challenge with the necessary software and peripherals.

REMEMBER

It starts with your computer. Are its specifications up to carrying your webinar? Most webinars are audio-only. But even if yours isn't, these days most laptops, iMacs, and MacBooks have a web camera, as seen in Figure 7-1, making it perfectly conceivable that you could hold a webinar while sitting at your desk, provided it's a relatively quiet room. If you plan on using video, flattering light helps too. Few people would notice where the webinar actually took place, and others would never care as long as there were no problems and it looked good.

Figure 7-1: The built-in webcam on a MacBook Pro.

When deciding on an effective spot for your next webinar, consider the following:

- **A nice quiet place:** You can hold a webinar just about anywhere, provided it's relatively quiet with enough space. Unless you have a major production, you don't need a sound stage. Depending on the type of webinar you're delivering, there's nothing wrong with a *little* office noise, but generally speaking, you need quiet. But if your space is adjacent to a construction site, high-traffic area, or a train yard, it's probably a good idea to find another spot.
- **Good lighting:** Quite simply, the better the lighting, the better you look. Good lighting also controls the color in the scene, taking it from a dominant cast or muted tone to vibrant color with good separation. We all know why people go to a professional photographer for important pictures instead of using the snapshots they post on Facebook. Part of that photographer's magic comes from good lighting. Maybe it doesn't matter that the look is less than perfect when you're using social media or communicating with FaceTime on your iPhone with your BFF, but nobody wants to see you or some expert talking to them with shadows across their face, or worse, under your eyes. (Disregard the latter if you're reaching out to the raccoon community.)

- **Clear sound:** Can you hear me now? It's not just a catchphrase, but also an issue and a concern that decides if your audience sticks around. Although your audience needs to see you clearly, it's equally, if not more, important that they hear you — the clearer, the better. That kind of sound quality doesn't happen easily and definitely not when you're depending on the pinhole microphone on your laptop, or with your mouth to the cell phone receiver. Instead, you should opt for a portable microphone, or better yet, use a clip-on or lavaliere microphone, as seen in Figure 7-2.

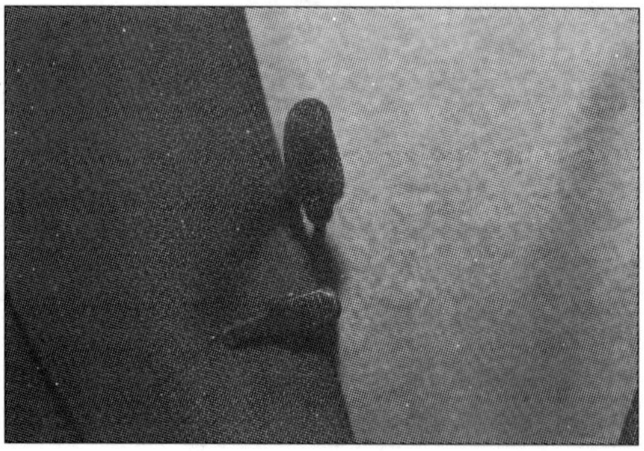

Figure 7-2: Lavaliere microphone clips to the speaker and takes up no additional space.

Using a studio

Sometimes the webinar is intimate enough that a single host can conduct the meeting from a small room, but other times, it's more expansive, requiring a much more spacious setup.

Regardless of the size of your presentation, there are a variety of reasons to using a dedicated studio. They range from wanting to properly decorate the set to providing a comfortable set for your interview-style webinar with some comfortable chairs or a couch and nice décor. Then, of course, there's the need for substantial space to conduct a moderated panel of guests.

In many of these situations — besides the space needed for talent — you also need to have just enough room for equipment, furniture, and people.

Realistically, there's no reason you wouldn't approach many of these situations the same way as a television shoot. That's because in many ways, an interview-style webinar or panel of guests is captured in the same way as a television news program.

Some webinar providers offer these facilities for a nominal fee or as part of their deluxe packages. Of course, that means that it may go beyond your budget. If you need to find a space to accommodate your vision but need to keeps cost down, look for your own professional space.

Here are the basic types of studios available for rental:

TIP

- **TV studio:** Almost every city has some sort of rentable television facility, whether it's a television production house or a local station maximizing revenue by renting out studio space, as seen in Figure 7-3, that's not being used at that time of day. They come in all shapes and sizes — or at least rectangular and square — to suit your specific needs. There are compact ones for your serious single-speaker chats, and more elaborate ones for your bigger, multi-camera webinar setup. Because they're already designed for television production, they include optimal lighting and audio controls, or at the very least, the right places to set them up. Some even provide the necessary connectivity for video conferencing, including Internet-based systems. Then there are the full-service facilities that provide cameras for a variety of situations and offer on-site support.
- **Audio studio:** Depending on how much space you need, you can rent out an audio studio for an hour or more. A place normally used for recording music at the very least gives you pristine audio (after all, that's what they're designed to do), and all the connections are there. It's also less expensive than renting a television facility. The biggest problem that you'll face is not being able to switch the video between cameras without bringing your own gear, or renting it for the occasion.
- **Photo studio:** Although booking a television recording studio can be pricey, a photo studio often offers a slightly less expensive rate. For the most part, it's a large empty space. You'll also have to bring your own technical gear and find out if there's a fast Internet connection.

Figure 7-3: A television production studio.

Other locations

Possible webinar locations cover a wide span, from the bare bones to grandiose. For a cozy webinar, you can sit at your desk with an iPad or laptop computer, controlling each aspect yourself and reaching as many people as you need. Outside of provider costs, the desktop webinar costs next to nothing to stage.

Then there's the other end of the spectrum, the full-tilt production. That usually calls for renting a large space to accommodate your dog and pony show with multiple speakers, a multiple camera setup, or a panel of guests. The more ambitious you get, the more you will propel your budget to the upper stratosphere. More power to you for being able to produce a grand session with all the bells and whistles, but then again, it's equally impressive when you go to the other extreme by just doing the basics.

REMEMBER

Somewhere in the middle of those two extremes lies the more common approach of finding a room that works for you. Maybe that means converting an empty space into a production area. Other times, it's about using your imagination to hold it in an exotic location, or at least someplace more interesting than a conference room or soundstage. So although the budget on this level is not always low, there's a sense of making the best out of your own resources to make things work for you.

That means you can hold your webinar in a variety of places that include

- **Conference room:** They already provide the look and feel of a banal office setting, as seen in Figure 7-4, so why not use them when appropriate? Other advantages of using a conference room include reliable connections, quiet and minimal interruptions, and distractions.
- **Office suite:** Whether it's in a single office, or a spot on the cube farm with cubicles as far as the eye can see, this scenario can work for you too.
- **Environmental setting:** Although it's radical, you can hold your webinar on location (hotel conference room, convention center, job fair, and so on), helping your audience see your webinar from an appropriate location.
- **Any empty space:** Whether it's a garage, warehouse, or an unused room, all it takes is a coat of paint, some furniture, and the proper equipment to create your version of *Extreme Webinar Space Makeover.*

Figure 7-4: Medium-sized conference rooms can work well for a small webinar, especially if you clear the room of all the chairs.

Connecting Your Technology

Equally important to securing a physical space is making sure that it has the necessary infrastructure to connect to the outside world. Obviously, electricity is the most basic need, so that rustic cabin in the woods that you bought as a getaway to party like it's 1899 probably won't work out.

WARNING! But it's not just electricity that matters. Sure, you need it to power the location, but there are situations when you can get away without having it, by using batteries, power packs, generators, and so on. The same cannot be said about an Internet connection. That's an essential part of the communication process, and the lifeline of the webinar. Not only do you need it, but you need to have a strong signal that is stable enough to sustain your entire session. Remember, if it drops out, so do participants.

WARNING! A weak connection or one that's unstable has the same effect as your seven-year-old self getting in the family car and pretending to drive someplace. A parked car in the driveway is acceptable for a kid with an imagination, but a webinar console with no Internet truly takes you nowhere. So be sure you have a strong web connection wherever you hold your next webinar.

Here's a rundown of what you'll need for connecting to your webinar at your location:

- **Modem/router:** Whether it's a hard-wired situation, a cellular one, or a Wi-Fi signal, it's what you need to breathe your message to the cyber world.

- **Computer:** Although obvious, it's necessary to mention. Make sure that it's an up-to-date model that can support all of the stuff you need to run a webinar.
- **Your presentation:** Make sure that your computer is loaded with the proper version of PowerPoint, and your presentation's slides are in the correct order.
- **Necessary peripherals:** This refers to everything else you need to carry on your webinar, from your video camera and audio equipment and perhaps a tin of Altoids.

Shooting video in a confined space

Many webinars use video, so it means you'll have to pick the type that best serves your needs. You also have the added worry of making sure the equipment fits in your designated space.

Many presentations use video from the built-in webcam on a laptop for video, or at least a clip-on model. The quality is not terrific, but seems to improve with every generation. These take up no more room than your computer, so space is not an issue.

REMEMBER

When you decide you need something more sophisticated like a separate camcorder on a tripod, either because you want better quality or need to pan to different speakers, space becomes an issue. Although this setup can provide the increased image quality and versatility that you'll need, it will also require a few more feet of real estate. Suddenly that room that was big enough for the single-presenter webinar is getting cramped. Then there are webinars that need the equivalent of a full television production set. You're not pulling that off in your corner office.

Regardless if you're going full-tilt with an elaborate set or bare bones in your closet, you need to be sure that your space can support your video needs. And remember: When it comes to lighting and sound capture, it's more than the size of the space that matters. It's also the physical attributes.

These include

WARNING!

- **Concrete wall and ceilings:** They reverberate sound and wreak havoc on audio quality. You can control this by using a lavaliere (clip-on) microphone and strategically placed sound baffles (sound-absorbing boards placed near the speaker) throughout the room, as seen in Figure 7-5.
- **Colorful walls:** They influence color balance in the scene — and rarely to your advantage — by reflecting color on the subject. Solutions include using a white bounce card on the opposite side of the subject and taking an accurate white-balance of the scene before shooting. See more about these topics in Chapter 12.

Figure 7-5: Sound-absorbing material helps audio quality.

TIP

- **Natural light from windows:** The soft light pouring into the room is great for capturing photographic portraits, but not as good when it comes to video, especially with the camera running for nearly an hour. Because sunlight constantly changes, it's not consistent enough for the entire webinar. In these situations, draw the curtains, or bring black plastic to tape over the windows. Just make sure it's not in the shot.

  If you're doing your webinar from a typical office building, use a room with no windows.

When it comes to using video at your webinar, you can do it a variety of ways. These include

- **Webcam:** Make sure that you have good, even lighting so that you look your best on camera.
- **Video camera:** Besides good lighting, be sure you have room to place the camera on a tripod in front of you. The camera should be at least five feet away from the subject.
- **Multi-camera:** This gets tricky because the amount of space required to pull it off increases substantially. Not only do you need enough room for the camera, but you also need to be sure that you can position the camera at an effective distance, so there's enough room to have a different perspective and angle with the second camera.
- **Video clips:** Some webinars don't use video for the presenter, but rely on video clips incorporated into a PowerPoint presentation. These require no extra room, and are quite effective for many situations.

Lighting

Somewhere between the unflattering look of restroom illumination and the vibrant glow of the hosts on your favorite morning news program lies the perfect look for your talking head. Now you may think that the lighting in your conference room or office looks pretty good, and it's entirely possible that you're right. But a more likely scenario is the available lighting that appears acceptable when you're walking around the office doesn't translate too well on camera. Overhead fluorescent lighting tends to produce unflattering color and shadows on the face, or has a wide light ratio that looks like the outfield at Wrigley Field in the mid-afternoon. By the way, that's when the scene shows both dark shadows and blown-out highlights. Either scenario provides more of a distraction than proper illumination.

Lighting video on a budget

You don't need a fancy lighting kit to effectively illuminate your presenter, nor do you need a lot of space to adequately light a simple situation. But as the presentation size increases, it's often necessary to consider more sophisticated lighting design. Although I discuss lighting more thoroughly in Chapter 12, for now, you need to consider locations that are big enough to not only support the speakers, but that also provide enough room for adequate lighting.

Consider the minimum space required to light each of the following scenarios:

- **Desktop:** A small light on the desk or podium can work, provided that the illumination isn't harsh.
- **Single speaker with video camera:** Be sure there's enough room in front of the speaker for a tripod-mounted camcorder, and at least one light on a stand next to it.
- **Multi-camera:** You'll obviously need a little more room to fit another camera, most likely on the opposite side of the room. Be sure your space can handle it.
- **Moderated panel:** This is the most challenging in terms of logistics because it's not much different than prepping for a television news show. You must be sure that each participant is properly illuminated, and that requires the lights to be effectively arranged. You'll also need enough room for at least one static camera and another to move freely on a dolly.

The light can be simple. Have a main light on your face at a 45-degree angle and a white bounce card out of camera range.

Audio

Although I discuss audio issues in detail in Chapter 12, here are a few audio aspects of your location to consider. These rules only apply to studio video presentations. Audio only webinars rely on a telephone line:

TIP

- **Cables:** You need them to connect to your computer, microphone, and camera, and they can become unwieldy if not kept in check. Be sure to not let cables become unmanageable; otherwise, they can turn your set into a high tech rat's nest. Although a simple microphone setup requires minimal control, a multi-camera or moderated panel will produce all sorts of lines across the floor. Make sure that loose cables are secured with Velcro floor cable covers, as seen in Figure 7-6, or by using gaffer tape.
- **Audio board:** If you have a sophisticated situation that requires an audio board on site, be sure that you consider space for it out of the way. Disregard this if the studio you're using is already equipped.
- **Microphone:** Make sure you have enough room to set up your microphones, especially if they're on a stand. Sometimes with a moderated panel, there's an audio person controlling a *boom mike*. (That's the one that's held overhead and looks like a fluffy squirrel on a stick.) If you're going that route, you may need some extra room to provide enough space to radially move the mike from speaker to speaker.
- **The room:** There's a big difference between capturing audio in a space with drywall and carpet and a room with a concrete floor and brick walls. The latter will surely present problems, and if you're on the low end of a budget, it's best to find a space more conducive to absorbing sound.

Figure 7-6: Velcro floor cable covers come in various lengths and are ideal for carpeted floors.

Putting It All Together

You can perform a webinar just about anywhere, but you still need to be conscious of your environment to carry it out effectively. Here's a checklist:

- **Find the right space:** Make sure it's the right fit for your needs.
- **Have a healthy Internet connection:** It's a deal-breaker if you cannot connect to the outside world.
- **Decide on a format:** Each webinar format has its own needs for space, so if you secured a spot for a single speaker, web-camera presentation, it's not feasible to try and do a moderated panel in the same place at the last minute.
- **Bring the right equipment:** Whether you rent it or bring your own, you need lights, microphones, and an appropriate computer. Otherwise, your audience won't see, hear, or experience your presentation, respectively. And don't forget to use a quality handset or headset as well.

Chapter 8

Practice, Practice, Practice

In This Chapter

- Preparing your material
- Getting comfortable with all the pieces
- Understanding how to engage your audience
- Rehearsing your webinar

Remember the old story about a young musician asking how to get to Carnegie Hall? Depending on how you perceive the question, you might tell him to walk down Third Avenue and make a left on 57th Street until he gets to Seventh Avenue, and then look up.

Or you could simply respond, "Practice."

Both answers are correct based on your position.

But here's the kicker. Regardless if you're a musical prodigy, baseball player, or a webinar producer, the latter answer remains true. If you're a violin virtuoso, your goal is to be one of the best who has ever played the instrument. That's not much different if you're a pitcher or shortstop, where skill builds over time. Hopefully, after an extended period of intense practice and competition, you're ready for the major leagues.

Seemingly, the webinar producer has a less lofty pursuit, yet it's equally important. At the end of the day, making sure that everything goes as planned with your online meeting is equally gratifying, not to mention a little easier than mastering a sport or difficult instrument (but only by a smidge).

Like a basic orchestration between a few instruments, the webinar has all sorts of moving pieces — some technical, others human — that need to work in unison to achieve success. It comes as no surprise that technical and human aspects are fickle at times and together can become exponentially chaotic. It's all about living on the fault line, from managing your Internet connection and handling issues with the webinar software to controlling the timing of each section and keeping the running times of different speakers in check. It doesn't take much imagination to see how problems can escalate rather quickly. So while the webinar producer doesn't face the same challenges as someone mastering an instrument, the goal of perfection is not much different.

Drawing from musical greatness, the surest way to make sure your webinar goes off with as few glitches as possible is to practice every aspect of it. Everything from getting the script right to creating the PowerPoint images to making sure the presenter and guests stick to their allotted time are all factors. Often, these factors could make or break the webinar.

So if you want to know how to make the perfect webinar, the answer is, "Practice, practice, practice."

Mastering Your Material

If you were a composer, your materials would include sheet music, as seen in Figure 8-1, and an arrangement for it too, as well as the supporting players and the venue to perform. That same structure applies to the webinar. Think about it. The script acts as the sheet music, whereas the itinerary is the arrangement. Then there are the players, which are the people associated with the webinar — from the speakers to support staff. The Internet acts as the place where it all plays out, just like Carnegie Hall, as seen in Figure 8-2. Clearly, practice makes perfect for both the musician and the webinar producer.

The script

Your script covers the written account of the webinar and can vary in structure and length. Whether you write a tightly written script that is followed to the letter by the presenter, or prefer a loose one that allows for some improvisation, it's important to practice it until it comes across as natural. Besides getting the delivery down pat, you do this to flesh out details to see what visual components work, or not, as well as the proper segue between each section. It's a good idea to read the script through the first time — regardless if you're the one who's delivering it — from start to finish while timing it with all the visual aids and sections.

Figure 8-1: Sheet music speaks to everyone in the band or orchestra, just as your webinar script lets everyone know their role and timing.

Figure 8-2: The famed Carnegie Hall

Consider the following:

- **Do a full dry run on your own:** If you have the time, and aren't sure if your script is working, go through the motions on your own before bringing others into it. This way, you can figure where to cut, where to expand, and which areas are flexible. Afterward, you can bring in your presenters and support staff for a full rehearsal.
- **Have your PowerPoint slides ready:** Rehearsal is a good time to make sure that your PowerPoint presentation works for the discussion. Although you shouldn't have so many slides that it's cumbersome and time-consuming to run, you should have your key images ready to make sure the whole event comes together well. Also, at this point, you can figure out where to add or cut slides.
- **Have effective segues in mind:** Transitioning from topics or to speakers takes some time, and when you add them up, they can take up a few minutes of the webinar. Don't forget to consider it when timing the session.

Itinerary

Although the script covers the actual presentation, it doesn't always take into account all of the other activity in the webinar. For example, if the script calls for speaker number two to come on for 10 minutes at the 25-minute mark, you need to make sure she is in position well before then. In addition, the itinerary takes into account all the pre-webinar stuff, from the invitations to the event itself, and the on-demand playback and follow-up.

Here's some of what the itinerary needs to cover:

- **What you promise:** Make sure that everything promised in the invitation is covered.
- **Keep to the schedule:** Remember, the schedule begins after the invitations go out and extends to when the link is sent out for replay.
- **Start to finish:** Try to plan everything from the invitation and registration to the time leading up to the webinar and follow-up with your audience.

Speakers

After the speaker is comfortable with the script and the supporting content, it's important to practice to sound comfortable and engaging. That happens through experience and practice. The speaker should be thoroughly comfortable with the material before the actual webinar.

Here are some areas to consider:

- **Rehearse the speaking part:** The speaker comes across as natural from understanding the material and rehearsing it.
- **Prepare for the Q&A:** Nothing is worse than not understanding a question or having the right response for it. That's why it's a good idea to anticipate potential questions in advance in order to respond quickly and accurately with concise answers.
- **Get the pronunciations right:** Saying a word correctly is often half the battle, so be sure to pronounce people's names, industry jargon, Latin phrases, and other complex words correctly. Messing up a word is enough to make people doubt your ability. If necessary, write words out phonetically so can remember how to pronounce them. Computer dictionaries include a phonetic spelling and definitions, and often an audio recording of pronunciation, as seen in Figure 8-3.

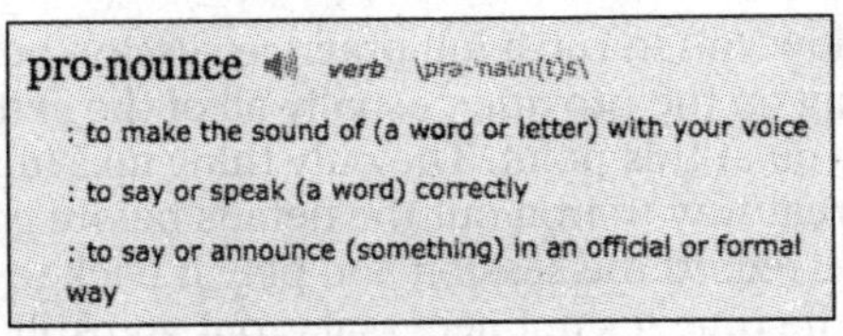

Figure 8-3: An example of a pronouncer found on common dictionary sites.

Support staff

Make sure that your support staff has a clear understanding of both the overall webinar topic and their specific tasks. Whether it's making sure that the connection stays up, moderating the event, or cueing the speakers, it comes together with practice. On the technical side, those folks should make sure everything is working, while being prepared to assist the audience, should they need to handle a question in the Q&A. When you're ready to perform a full-blown rehearsal, be sure that everyone involved on the big day is part of the practice session.

Here are some ideas to consider for your team members:

- **Dedicate a timekeeper:** It's not a bad idea to use a stopwatch, as seen in Figure 8-4, to make sure the rehearsal goes well. If you're not the timekeeper, dedicate someone on your team to be one.
- **Monitor the speaker:** It's important for everyone to listen to the speaker for a variety of reasons, including making sure the discussion is on track, that the slides are correct, and that the speakers run on time.

Figure 8-4: No problem if you don't have a separate stopwatch. Most smartphones either include one, or have an app for it.

Webinar service providers

Some service providers allow you to run a full practice session before the actual start time. Depending on the provider, usually all of the settings and features are accessible to you at this point. The only thing missing are the attendees, making this a great way to iron out the details before going live. If you have enough lead time, record the session and play it back to see where you can improve. Most of the time it's not necessary, but you still have that luxury if you want to get it just right.

Timing

Because the webinar has a time constraint, mentioned right on your invitation, it's important that you stick with it. Even if your webinar runs for 55 minutes, it's important to plan out a schedule for each segment, so that it doesn't go 60. Making sure that each covers its allotted time is essential.

So be sure to do the following:

- **Start promptly, sort of:** You want to start on time, but it's a good idea to actually wait one or two minutes to actually start talking to account for latecomers. Instead, use that time to welcome your audience and tell them you'll be getting started shortly. Or just let them listen to the snappy music that is provided with the platform.
- **Make an introductory statement about the technology:** Take a minute to explain the controls and interaction options.
- **Vary speaker times:** Whether you have a single speaker or several speakers, try to limit each talking session to 10-20 minutes. You can break it up with a poll, and then go back to the speaker.
- **Save time for Q&A:** The question-and-answer portion of the show is what ties it all together. In an hour-long webinar, you should allocate at least ten minutes to this period.

Engagement

Engaging your audience is every bit as important as the content that you provide to them. And with webinars, it's more important than ever. In the brick-and-mortar world, you've probably had the misfortune of attending a really boring meeting, but you were part of a captive audience and couldn't leave without being seen.

It's entirely different when the meeting is online. The audience can easily log off, walk away from their computer or do something else, and you will not be the wiser. That makes their engagement your first priority, so be sure to work on techniques that keep them interested.

Consider the following:

- **Know your audience well:** The better you know your audience, the more that you can understand their needs and that your content is relevant to them. You can get an idea from the time that they register, and modify what you know through chat and polling during the webinar.

- **Have interesting slides:** The visual portion of the show solidifies your point, so give your audience something worthwhile to concentrate on.
- **Get personal:** Depending on the size and nature of the webinar, feel free to mention some of the registrants by calling out their names, when appropriate.
- **Entertain them:** You're there to inform your audience, but you can entertain them as well. Give them reasons to stay logged on with a compelling yet personable host. In addition, the speaker and visual aids should also piqué their interest.

Flow

Think of your webinar much like you would a new recipe. You have assembled all of the ingredients; now it's time to make them all come together.

Like cooking, the webinar is much more than the sum of its parts. And also like cooking, it won't turn out right if you don't put your best into it. In a seven-course meal, the food and wines all complement one another to create a culinary flow. Well, guess what? The success of your webinar also depends on flow. From presenter to slides to speaker to Q&A, the whole event should ebb and flow like an ocean tide, as seen in Figure 8-5.

Figure 8-5: The Pacific Ocean tide shows its ebb and flow.

But flow isn't always something you can control, although when it happens, it's a beautiful thing.

To improve your chances, you should practice each part of your webinar, separately and together. Consider the following during your practice sessions:

- **Speak up before the speaking begins:** The host and speakers play a big part in making sure the show moves along nicely while informing and entertaining the audience, but all that begins at the planning stage. Be sure to pick interesting, skilled speakers and have a good script for them (no matter who writes it).

- **Time management:** Although it's not show business, you still want to keep the audience wanting more, so after each section makes its point, be sure to keep the show moving. Practice helps you and your team set a comfortable pace that hopefully avoids any awkward transitions.
- **Pace the content:** Switch it up between passive listening and active participation. For example, after your first speaker, break things up a bit by switching gears. You can send the audience a poll to complete or show a video clip. Maintaining flow often deals with this type of tempo.
- **Keep the boring stuff in check:** Sometimes it's necessary to provide the audience with announcements, disclaimers, and technical information. Just try to drop it in sparingly. In other words, don't say it all at once; otherwise, it will act as a buzz-kill to your webinar.

Testing Your Equipment

Although it seems like a no-brainer, you'd be surprised how often producers assume their equipment is working correctly, but are unpleasantly surprised when something doesn't work as expected. So don't just practice the content of your webinar, but make sure everything else is working too. Many webinar service providers allow you to do a full test run that only you can see. You should check the following to make sure that it's fully operational:

- **Webinar software:** Take it for a test drive in the rehearsal mode.
- **Widgets:** Make sure everything associated with software is working correctly, like the polling and Q&A interfaces.
- **Video equipment:** Whether you're using the built-in webcam on your MacBook Air, using a small HD camcorder as seen in Figure 8-6, or planning a multi-camera shoot, make sure that all the gear is fully operational.

Figure 8-6: Though compact, an affordable 3CCD HD camcorder can yield impressive results.

- **PowerPoint:** Making sure the program is fully operational is obvious, but also be sure that you have enough hard disk space and RAM for it to run smoothly. In addition, be sure that there are no conflicts with other software. Better yet, it's a good idea to only run the applications that you need and make sure you have only one PowerPoint presentation open. Of course, you'll have fewer worries if the presentation is already uploaded before the webinar.

Rehearsing the Event

Make sure that your rehearsals run as close as possible to what you have in the script and itinerary and plan for areas that run slightly longer or shorter than anticipated.

Some webinar producers conduct a full dress rehearsal, replete with different scenarios long before the outside world gets to experience it, but that's often overkill. Realistically, if you feel confident with the structure of your webinar, you should practice the delivery and content before you run it live.

That doesn't negate going all-out on a dress rehearsal ahead of your webinar. There are simply too many reasons not to perform a full practice session. That's because each of those reasons are like little fires that need extinguishing when nobody is looking. It's all a matter of how comfortable you are with delivering the material.

Treat the session as the real thing and use your employees, friends, or other trusted folks as your audience. Have them be on the lookout for the good, the bad, and the ugly. Before the webinar, poll them to see what modifications you should make before going live.

Here's what your staff/audience should look for when watching your webinar:

- **Technical issues:** Have them check whether the video is clear, and be sure that the audio quality is not too low, over-modulated, or subject to some kind of interference. Also, make sure that the polls and Q&A are working properly. Glitches occur regularly, but if you can catch some early, now is the time.
- **Speaker performance:** Your test audience should carefully critique the performance of the host and speakers, making sure they sound natural and knowledgeable. They should also determine whether the speaker holds their interest, whether he is talking too fast or too slow, and whether the pace is comfortable to follow.

- **Visual presentation:** It's important to determine whether the PowerPoint presentation nicely complements the host and speakers, or whether it does at all. Are there too many slides? Too few? And are they up long enough, but not too long? These are all valid points that you can discover in the rehearsal.
- **Content:** Does the webinar address everything that it promised in the invitation? If not, now is the time to modify before the big day.

Chapter 9

Getting the Word Out

In This Chapter

- Publicizing your webinar
- Constructing an e-mail invitation
- Bolstering your database
- Using Twitter, Facebook, and other social media
- Demanding on-demand

"Extra, extra! Read all about it!"

Funny how those newsboys hawking the newspaper headlines were pretty effective when it came to selling papers on the street. Of course, that was early in the twentieth century before television and the Internet came into the picture. In those days, newspapers were the main source of information, so barking the headlines clearly sold papers, at least more than the passive approach of waiting for pedestrians to come over and ask what was in the news.

Times have obviously changed, but the importance of letting people know what you have to offer hasn't. Remember, just as newspaper sales were once very important, the same holds true for attendance to your webinar these days. The effectiveness of the presentation depends on many factors, but getting the appropriate audience — regardless of size — is paramount.

But how can you best promote your upcoming webinar? You can't go out in the village square — or its modern equivalent, the shopping mall — while holding an iPad and scream the virtues of your upcoming session. (Well, you can, but I wouldn't recommend it.) Best-case scenario, you'll get a few stares. The worst-case scenario could lead to a stint in mall jail with an inebriated Santa Claus.

Yet that turn-of-the-century newsboy charm does have its place when it comes to promoting your next online soiree. You can't stand on a street corner, though. Instead, you have to reach out to the masses through the modern equivalent of the populated square: the online space. People are always on their computers and smartphones, and because the webinar takes place via the Internet and is seen on computers — or any other type of web-enabled device — that makes cyberspace the new town square.

That sounds like a no-brainer. After all, how hard can it be to draw a large group of people to your webinar, especially when most of the time the event is free? Well, you may be in for a rude awakening. With so much content on the web, most people won't even know you're presenting a webinar, let alone that it may include subject matter that they'd be interested in.

REMEMBER

Clearly, your first objective is to let them know you have a webinar that suits their interest. Your second goal is to get them to sign up. Not everyone is going to be looking for you, so you can't wait for them to come to you.

In this chapter, I explore the various methods of letting them know what you have to say.

Publicizing Your Event

After you've abandoned the idea of shouting about the virtues of your webinar in a public place, it's important to find some other ways to get the job done. That's great because there are some really effective methods of promoting your upcoming event that do not embarrass your kids at the mall. Successful webinar promotion tends to happen in at least one of three ways: web advertising, social media, and e-mail. Sure, there are other approaches, but the most effective use the Internet to reach and inform their audience.

These methods are not created equal, however. Each offers varying degrees of effectiveness depending on your needs, the segment of the market represented, and what you're looking to tell them.

TIP

E-mail remains a rock star when it comes to reaching an audience. Sending e-mail invitations works across the board for getting the word out and bringing recipients to your registration page. Facebook, Twitter, LinkedIn, and Google+ can work to some degree on their own, but all act as an adjunct to the e-mail notification. Social media platforms do have some hold in their respective markets. For example, business-to-business organizations will often use e-mail notification to get word out, but supplement with LinkedIn.

Using e-mail notifications: The numero uno tool

REMEMBER

Not every computer-savvy person uses social media, but just about everyone who uses a computer has an e-mail account. Even Grandma has a Gmail account these days, so it's obvious that e-mail marketing is an important mechanism for letting people know about your upcoming webinar. It makes perfect sense to send out an e-mail blast.

Sounds simple, right? Maybe, but getting the user to open and read your message is only the first objective. The invitation should include a link or a button that the user clicks to bring them to a registration page. They can read about the webinar and potentially sign up for it. Think about it: It's a lot easier than screaming at the top of your lungs at the mall.

Just don't think it's as easy as flipping through your old Rolodex — er, that old-fashioned wheel of names and addresses, as seen in Figure 9-1. Using e-mail is a bit more sophisticated than sending out missives from a Rolodex or a little black address book. Delivering your message for an upcoming webinar often requires some marketing or e-mail automation. Instead of using an address book, e-mail automation depends on a database of names that lets you send out invitations to some or all the names in the database.

Here are some reasons why e-mail marketing works:

- **Just about everybody has an e-mail account:** *Almost* everyone has one, so that makes it more accessible than any other form of media, and more timely than sending an invitation through snail mail.
- **It's highly targeted:** You can send e-mails to those likely to be most interested in your message.
- **It's affordable:** While you might have to purchase lists, other costs are negligible.
- **It's ecologically sound:** The e-mail option saves trees because you're not using paper to print.

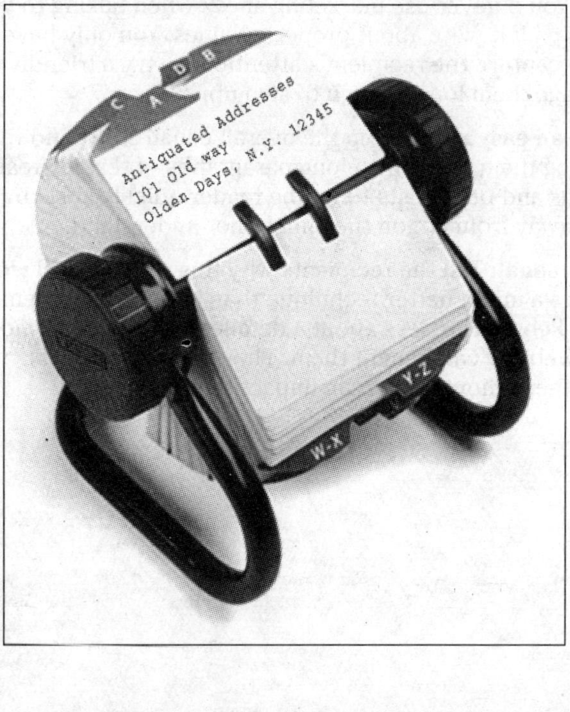

Figure 9-1: A Rolodex with a uniquely appropriate address for the webinar age.

Successfully connecting with potential attendees

It's easy to confuse the idea of reaching your potential audience with the act of *connecting* with them. That's why it's important to construct a convincing invitation to your next webinar. It's a shame to get recipients to open your e-mail only to find they were confused by your message and trashed it. Or maybe the webinar was suitable for their needs, but they passed anyway because you neglected to convey that.

Whatever the situation, here are a few tips for writing your e-mail invitation:

- **Accurately target the right people:** It's essential to reach the right individuals, so send invitations to those that fit the profile for the webinar, and not everyone on your e-mail list.
- **Have them at hello:** If you want a potential registrant to consider signing up, you must grab them with your subject line. Unlike most junk mail in the physical world, an unsolicited e-mail can still grab the attention of the recipient if the subject line is interesting. The subject line must be concise and engaging.
- **Dazzle them:** Getting a recipient to open the e-mail is the first step, with the next one being sure that the description of your upcoming webinar appeals to them enough that they will click the registration button.
- **Leave the business-speak for parodies:** Your e-mail should have a conversational tone. Pretend you're talking to a friend and not a business colleague. You'd never use marketing-speak when talking to your neighbor Rob, even if it were about property values. You only have a brief moment to capture the recipient's attention, so try a friendly approach. It may engage them long enough to sign up.
- **Give them an easy read:** Keep the overall e-mail short and resist the desire to bog them down with long paragraphs of text. Instead, use short descriptions and bullet lists to let the reader quickly absorb the message. Stay away from jargon they might not understand.
- **Make it personal:** Tell the recipients why this webinar will work for them. That's a much better technique than bombarding them with talking points. People care less about a detailed topic list and more about how your webinar can benefit them. They're more apt to sign up if you clearly let them know how it can impact them.

- **Proofread:** Read it repeatedly. Mistakes in grammar and layout look amateurish and can dissuade a reader from going further.
- **Stay focused:** Have a singular idea and stick with it. Don't pollute the page with content that doesn't support the theme; otherwise, it can look like the four-letter word of e-mail marketing: spam.

Writing the webinar invitation

Now that you're stoked about your upcoming webinar, it's time to let your audience know about it. Not only should you tell them when it's held, but also more importantly, you need to convince them that their presence can benefit them. This involves writing a compelling invitation, as seen in Figure 9-2, that involves the vital information of who, what, when, and where, but also how it can make their lives better.

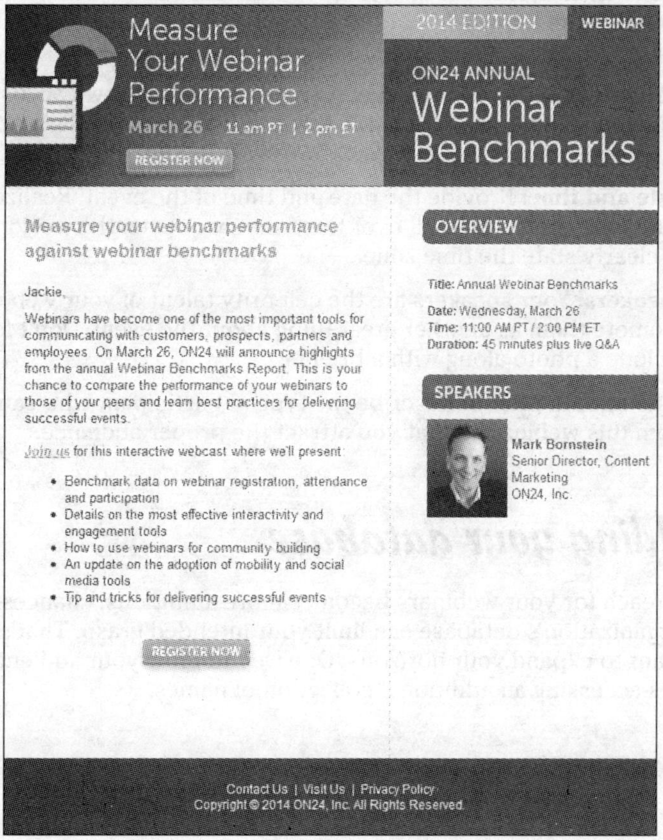

Figure 9-2: A webinar invitation should also convince the invitee to register for the webinar.

Organize your contacts

Before sending a single e-mail, take the time to organize your contacts. Make sure the proper fields are filled out and that the information is up-to-date.

Here's what each invitation should include:

TIP

- **Webinar title:** Here's a place where the age-old question of "What's in a name?" comes into play. If you're webinar has a humdrum title, people are going to pass it up quicker than they do a guy with a cough on the subway. Make sure your title uses active language that engages the reader.
- **Brief description:** If a title grabs their attention, it's the description that draws them closer to registering. In this short blurb, tell them in the friendliest of tones why this webinar works for them and what they can get out of it.
- **Obligatory bulleted message:** As readers, we've grown accustomed to bulleted summaries, so include three to five points outlining the webinar's benefits.
- **Date and time:** Provide the date and time of the event. Realize that registrants may come from all over the country or even the world, so be sure to clearly state the time zone.
- **Speakers:** Your speakers are the celebrity talent of your webinar, so promote them as another great thing about the event. Don't forget to include a photo along with a brief bio.
- **Who should attend:** Describe the type of participant who can benefit from this webinar so that you attract the proper audience.

Building your database

As the reach for your webinars becomes more ambitious, chances are that your organization's database can limit your intended grasp. That's why it's important to expand your horizons. One way to grow your audience base involves accessing an additional collection of names.

Before going any further, let me summarize. A database is like the modern equivalent of an address book, and a pretty detailed one at that. This organized collection becomes your pool for inviting people to your webinar. Made up of customers, contacts, and people associated with your industry, sometimes it draws directly from your customer profiles, whereas other times, it comes from social media followers such as those from LinkedIn. Twitter and Facebook friends, fans, and followers also add to the mix. And yet, sometimes that's not enough.

Sometimes, to attract a wider swath of potential registrants, you need to look elsewhere. That's because it's hard to grow when you constantly draw from your own database, especially when your database is relatively small. When you need to expand your list of contacts, you can build your database in a variety of ways to match your needs. Services are available that provide access to additional contacts for your invitation list for a fee. These act like the modern version of the mailing lists that companies used to purchase so they could direct-market their products. While you can find ways to bolster your own database, you can also purchase names, much like direct marketers used to buy mailing lists.

Here are some places to get names for your database:

- **Database.com:** A powerful, scalable cloud database for building social and mobile applications, as seen in Figure 9-3. Pricing begins at free and climbs steadily based on your needs and your number of users.

  For more information, go to `www.database.com/`.
- **Central Address Systems:** Provides e-mail lists for consumers and other market segments. Pricing varies based upon your needs.

  For more information, go to `www.cas-online.com/`.
- **ZoomInfo:** A vertical search engine with a database containing more than 95 million profiles of business professionals.

  For more information, go to `www.zoominfo.com`.
- **NetProspex:** NetProspex is another marketing database that provides leads to help B2B (business-to-business) marketers improve their contact data.

  For more information, go to `www.netprospex.com/`.

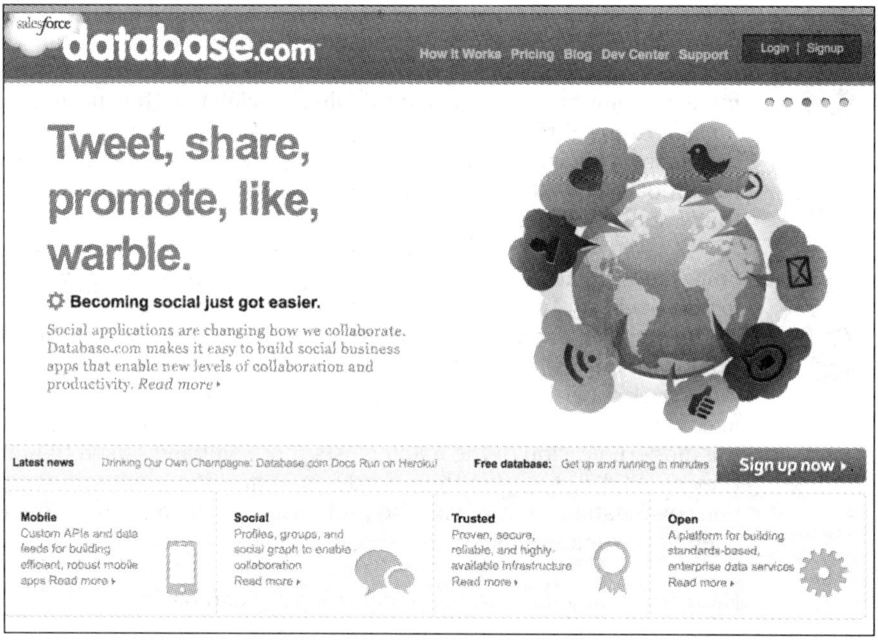

Figure 9-3: The Database.com website.

Relying on e-mail automation software

Writing a successful e-mail invitation means very little if you can't blast it out to the masses. Webinar producers often use some form of a marketing or e-mail automation platform to send out an invitation to some or all of their database. Automation programs typically handle the function of e-mailing a list from your database to potential registrants.

Popular e-mail programs include

- **MailChimp:** Lets you send out an e-mail blast about your upcoming webinar with reach of anywhere from 100 to 50,000 subscribers. This platform offers more than 400 templates, with many optimized for display on mobile devices. It will also allow you to summarize sent e-mail with a report on the number of opens, clicks, unsubscribes, and complaints your message received, as seen in Figure 9-4.

  For more information, go to www.mailchimp.com.

- **Emma:** If design qualities are important to you, this service includes around 40 templates and also offers fee-based custom design services.

Emma integrates with various social media sites as well as Google Analytics. You can also learn about e-mail activity with Emma's response-reporting feature that lets you view subscribers that took a particular action such as opening the e-mail or clicking on its links. It also integrates with Facebook.

For more information, go to `www.emma.com`.

- **Eloqua:** Eloqua (see Figure 9-5) is a sophisticated marketing automation platform that combines social media, marketing, and e-commerce solutions to help target the right buyers in the B2B world. The company was recently acquired by Oracle, further supporting its solid market footing.

  For more information, go to `www.eloqua.com`.

- **Marketo:** Covers all phases of marketing your webinar, including the ability to build automated customer engagement and nurture flows, detailed analysis features, and of course, the ability to create an e-mail campaign in a matter of minutes. It lets users send them out in batches, or triggered in real-time based on behaviors.

  For more information, go to `www.marketo.com`.

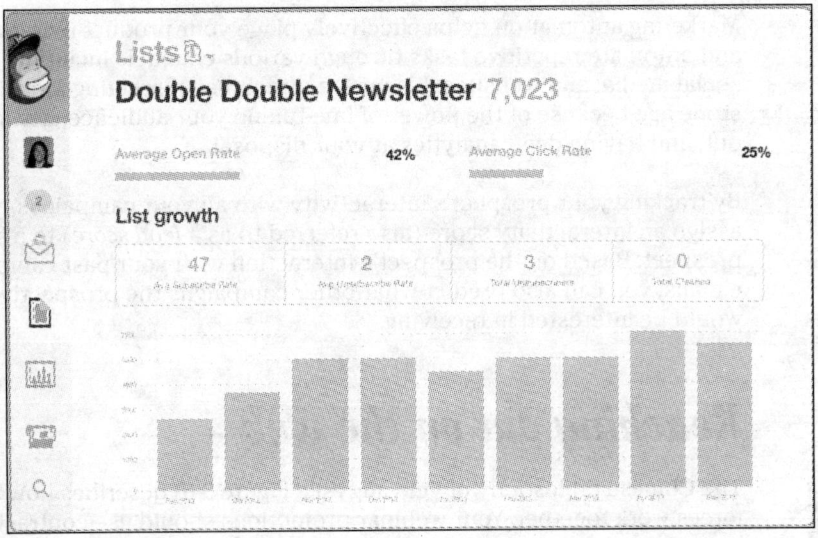

Figure 9-4: A chart from the MailChimp website.

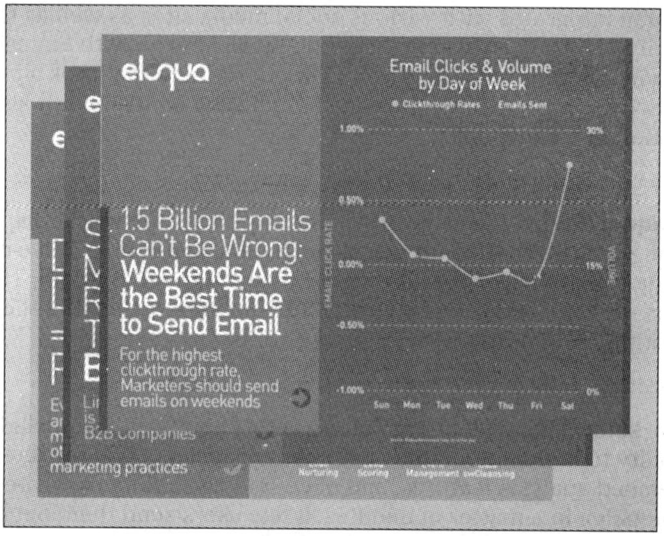

Figure 9-5: Eloqua provides a variety of tools and graphics on their website.

Using marketing automation

Marketing automation helps effectively place your product message online and automate repetitive tasks through various channels including email, social media, and websites. It's makes direct mail marketing look like the stone age because of the power of fine-tuning your audience, getting it right out, and having deep analytics at your disposal.

By tracking your prospect's interactivity with all your campaigns, you can assign an interactivity score (also referred to as a *lead score*) to a specific prospect. Based on the prospect's interaction with your past campaigns and e-mails, you can also predict what other campaigns the prospective viewer would be interested in receiving.

Reaching out on the web

The Chinese philosophy of yin-yang (see Figure 9-6) describes how contrary forces work together. Your webinar promotions should use contrasting forces as well: Both active and passive promotions are necessary to spread the word. The former refers to the active role of reaching your audience through e-mail, and the latter refers to the more passive approach of promoting your webinar using online resources.

Figure 9-6: The yin-yang symbol illustrates how seemingly opposite forces are interconnected.

Web advertising, in whatever form you choose, still requires the potential viewer to click a banner advertisement or go to your website on their own. It's remarkably similar to fishing, but it provides another means of bringing guests to the webinar.

Your web page is where people are directed to register, so make sure you create enough places online that direct potential participants to your page. In addition, web presence creates another opportunity to sign up viewers.

Here are some of the ways to use the web to promote your webinar:

- **Banner advertisements:** Because these ads can appear just about anywhere, they provide a means for reaching folks outside those on your e-mail list or purchased database. The banner lives on the service provider's server and from there is embedded on different web pages. You have to pay for this type of advertising, but the cost is minimal. Besides, you should always allocate part of your budget for paid advertising.
- **Your own website:** Directing traffic to your webinar's landing page provides another avenue to increase participation in your webinar. Visitors come from a number of places, including return visitors, e-mail notification, and social media. It's not a bad idea to use your own website or blog as ground zero for information. After all, there's no limit to how much information and detail you can include on your own site, and by detail, I mean images, graphics, and extended bios.
- **Syndication:** Never underestimate the power of using a partner to promote your webinar. For example, if you're planning a session on tips for flipping houses, consider partnering up with a real estate site (perhaps in exchange for mentioning them at your webinar) to help promote it. This can promote additional visibility to a receptive audience.

Placing notices in print media

Once the most powerful means of advertising, print media has been relegated to the shadows, at least when it comes to advertising in the online space. That's because the cycle times associated with online communications move much faster than those associated with print media.

For print such as *Advertising Age* and *Chief Learning Officer* magazine, the lead times are usually not conducive to advertising your webinar. For example, magazines are put together so far in advance that by the time your ad runs, your webinar is likely over.

TIP

Print is not dead when it comes to advertising your webinar, but you'll probably want to take a different approach. Instead of promoting a particular webcast, promote an online listing of all your webcasts. For example, you can advertise your landing page, and when the reader goes to that URL, they can view the Upcoming Events section of the page. So every time they go to that page, they see your current webinar and those coming up. Here are some tips for using print media to get the word out about your webinar:

- **Be opportunistic:** Use various forms of media to advertise your webinars, taking into consideration the longer cycle time of print media.
- **Advertise your site:** Webinars may come and go before the ad runs in print, but your website won't. Let users know what you have to offer and encourage them to visit.

News releases and media alerts

Another avenue to promote your webinar involves sending out a media alert or a news release. These share similarities with an e-mail invitation, except instead of going to the participants, it's released to the media and blogs. It lets them know there's something they should consider covering, and lets your industry know what you're doing.

REMEMBER

Although a news release and a media alert seem like the same thing, they are very different. Like its title suggests, a *media alert* lets a reader know something that's about to take place (for example, alerting its recipients of your upcoming webinar). Conversely, news releases provide additional information about your program and objectives. They can also discuss what you have coming up. Hopefully, a media outlet will do a short story or cover some aspect of your webinar. Often an editor will even attend a webinar, to experience the event first-hand.

Using Social Media

REMEMBER

E-mail notifications act as the primary means of finding your audience, but social media complements them by allowing you to communicate with your audience before, during, and after the webinar. And isn't that the key to all relationships? Whether they're friendship, marriage, or business, the key to keeping them strong lies in how well you communicate. The cyber world does it through social media. It lets you whisper your message to the world, and the best part is that you don't have to know everyone.

Promote your webinar across Facebook, Twitter, LinkedIn, and even Google+. Each of these social media platforms allows you to reach a different cross-section of users. But be aware that not all social media is created equal. Choosing the most effective one for your specific needs is key, but it depends on a variety of factors. These include the audience base that you're looking to appeal to and the field that you do business in.

Facebook

Facebook, as seen in Figure 9-7, is the most popular social networking platform on the planet, yet sometimes folks overlook its business potential. It's easy to see why. It seems everyone from 13 to 93 uses it purely for socializing with friends and family, but that reach of more than a billion users around the world offers a lot of potential.

TIP

With recent changes to its algorithm, corporate posts are reaching only 1–2% of a company's "likes." To reach your targets on Facebook, you have to sponsor your content — in other words, you have to pay Facebook to show it to people.

When it comes to webinars, Facebook does lag slightly behind Twitter and LinkedIn, (simply because some businesses use them more) but rises in importance depending on who you are and how you do business. For example, if you're a direct-to-consumer company, you might have a big Facebook presence, as opposed to business-to-business vendors that might prefer LinkedIn.

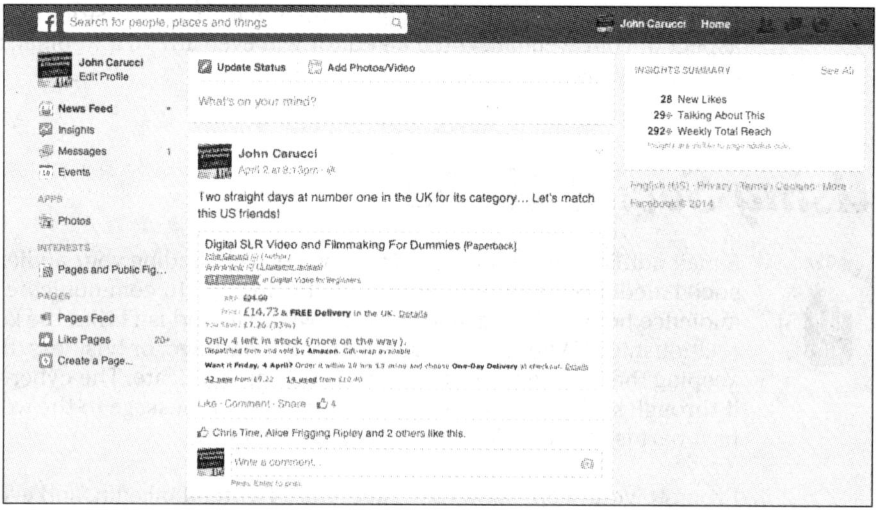

Figure 9-7: The very recognizable color and font of Facebook.

When you Facebook, consider the following:

- **Share your posts:** Post your webinar info and updates often so that potential participants see them.
- **Create a fan page:** Although Facebook requires users to approve their friends, when you set up a fan page, anyone who sees it can become a fan on their own just by Liking the page. This puts the page content on their newsfeed, so they'll be aware of your upcoming webinar. Of course, you can boost the amount of likes by paying Facebook to guarantee a specific number of likes.
- **Promote a Facebook Event:** Facebook lets you create invitations to events that can reach a public, private, or limited audience. Birthday parties, personal milestones, and oh yeah, your upcoming webinar can all take advantage of the Event feature. The more replies that come for friends that Like your Event, or mention that they're going, the more aware their friends become of your webinar.
- **Advertise on Facebook:** Facebook offers a fee-based plan, as seen in Figure 9-8, that allows you to advertise across the social networking site with a charge based on the number of clicks your ad gets. You can set a per-day cap to manage your budget. You can target these ads pretty tightly and see how many participants RSVP through them.

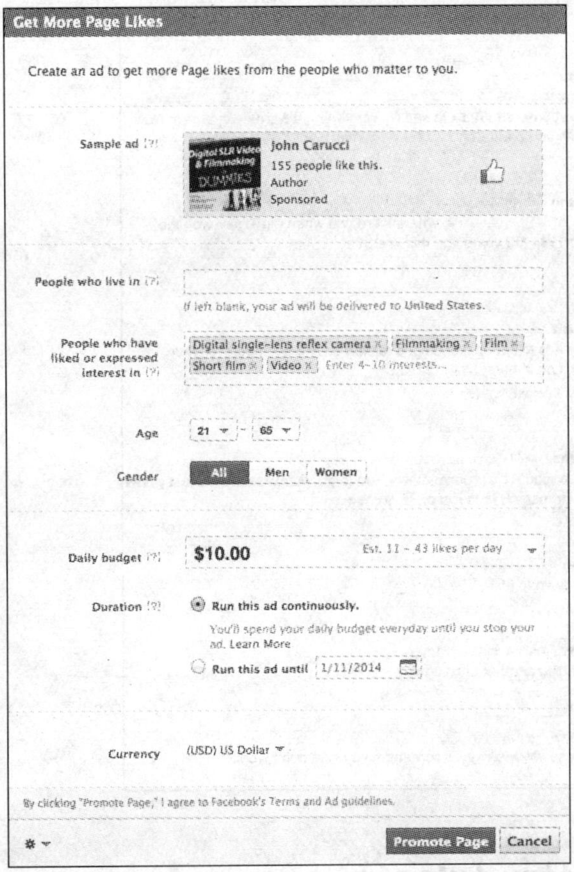

Figure 9-8: Facebook advertising is fairly simple and lets you set a budget for each day.

Twitter

If e-mail is the undisputed invitation champion, then Twitter, as seen in Figure 9-9, reigns supreme when it comes to staying in touch. Rock stars, actors, journalists, and companies all enjoy communicating with the world via the 140-character message. It's short, sweet, and often acts as the shot heard around the world. (If you're not sure about that one, just do a Google search of scandals involving comments posted by professional athletes and politicians.) The positive side of that is Twitter's incredible potential. In the business realm, Twitter is a popular marketing channel with both business-to-business marketers as well as those that go direct-to-consumer.

Figure 9-9: The very recognizable color and font of Twitter.

How Twitter tweets

Twitter lets you send short messages — no more than 140 characters — to people who follow you. In most cases, someone can follow you just by clicking the Follow button on your profile summary. They can also see your profile while they're searching for a topic. Some users manually approve their followers, but for business, that's a silly extra step.

Your 140-character messages can also include a link to a website or blog post, as well as a video or a picture. (And no, in this case, a picture doesn't count as 1,000 words.) People can not only read your tweets, but they can also reply, retweet (sharing your message by tweeting your tweet to their followers), or favorite it. (*Favoriting* lets your followers know they like your tweet. Tweets that you favorite are also collected in a special tab of your profile.)

Here's a look at some Twitter lingo:

- **Tweet:** The act of sending a 140-character message via Twitter, with or without photos, video, or a link. Or, such a message sent via Twitter.
- **Retweet:** Sharing a message originally from another person with your followers.
- **Favorite:** A method of letting followers approve of your tweet by designating it a favorite.
- **At (@) sign:** The symbol that precedes all Twitter handles. When you add the full Twitter handle to any tweet, everyone who follows that person will see the tweet. This differs from a hashtag, which can be seen by anyone searching for that topic.
- **Hashtag:** A spaceless summary of a tweet that is preceded by the pound sign (#). A hashtag acts as label for a topic and allows other users to find content by searching for that hashtag. For example, #FootballSunday can be added to tweets about NFL games on Sunday. Adding a hashtag allows the tweet to be seen by more people than when using the at sign because that only is seen by people who follow that handle.
- **Verified:** An official designation, as seen in Figure 9-10, provided by Twitter that helps users verify the authenticity of accounts for businesses and public figures. It's denoted by a blue check mark.
- **Trending:** The description of a phrase or topic that grows at a fast rate. For example, a major news event or a comment from a public figure can "trend" if lots of people are mentioning it or retweeting about it all at once.

Figure 9-10: The blue check mark of approval, better known as being verified as the real thing by Twitter.

Now that you have a lay of the land, here are some things to consider when tweeting about your webinar:

- **Tweet away:** Tweets don't build up in the user's inbox, so feel free to tweet as much as you feel is necessary. Start with the occasional tweet a few weeks before your webinar and tweet more heavily as time draws near.
- **Ask followers to retweet:** Industry colleagues, partners, and friends can extend the life and reach of a tweet.
- **Use a hashtag:** In addition to using the obligatory #webinar hashtag (that finds all webinars in a user search), feel free to use one that describes your webinar. For example, if your webinar is about designing effective blogs, use something like #blogdesign, or even the webinar name, if it fits.

LinkedIn

LinkedIn is a social networking website, as seen in Figure 9-11, for people in professional occupations who want to network. In some ways, it acts as an old-fashioned Rolodex on steroids. Like Facebook and Twitter, it's relatively easy to sign up for LinkedIn. Users create a profile that shares details about their education, work experience, and proficiencies. From that information, users can create a network of people from their education background, professional similarities, and colleagues, past and present. Here are some benefits to signing up for LinkedIn:

- **Stay in touch:** Provides a realistic way for users to stay in touch with former colleagues and schoolmates.
- **Network:** Increase your "schmooze" factor without ever getting out of your chair.
- **Job hunt:** Look for suitable companies when it's time to job-hunt, and equally as important, allow some of those headhunters to find you.
- **Find vendors:** The bigger your list of contacts, the more access you have to companies, vendors, and other qualified people.

LinkedIn can also help you spread the word about your business ventures, — in this case, that refers to your webinar. Like Facebook, it also lets you create an Event and advertise.

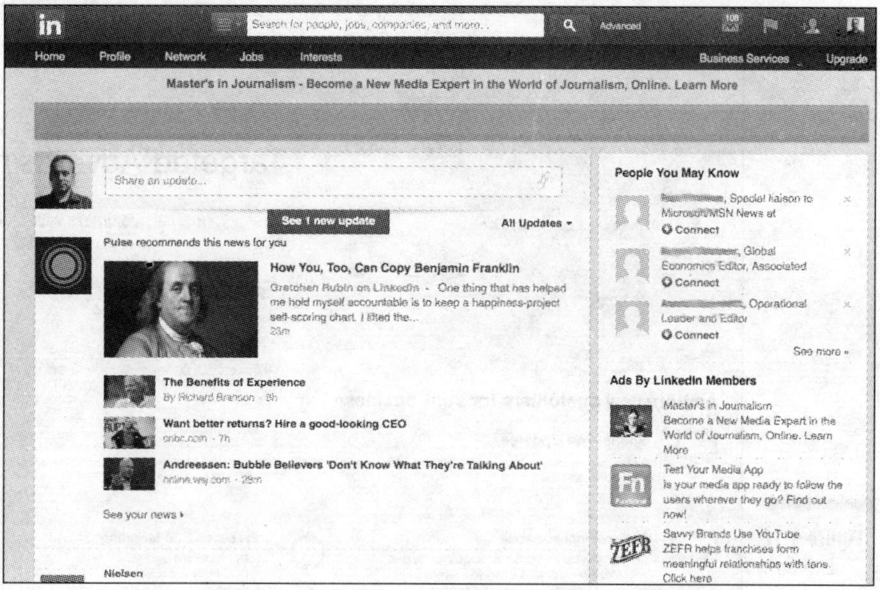

Figure 9-11: LinkedIn is networking for professionals.

Targeted advertising on LinkedIn

TIP

LinkedIn provides access to its 250 million users with its own advertising program that provides a great deal of flexibility. Unlike other social media sites, LinkedIn, as seen in Figure 9-12, lets you target specific business users and groups. Advertising on the social media platform is a bit more expensive than other forms of social media, but its reach and analytics may justify the cost for your webinar.

If you think it can work for you, here are some of the benefits:

- **Professional audience:** LinkedIn lets you connect with the world's largest audience of active, influential professionals. Launch your campaign in minutes. All you need is a LinkedIn account.
- **Sponsored updates:** They allow your business to promote your services to people and companies that are outside of your followers. You can even target who sees the message. Sponsored updates help build relationships and raise brand awareness across the web.
- **Precision B2B targeting:** You can hone in on the right people by filtering for job title, industry, company size, and other criteria.
- **Set your own budget:** There are no commitments or long-term contracts, and you can pay by the clicks or impressions.

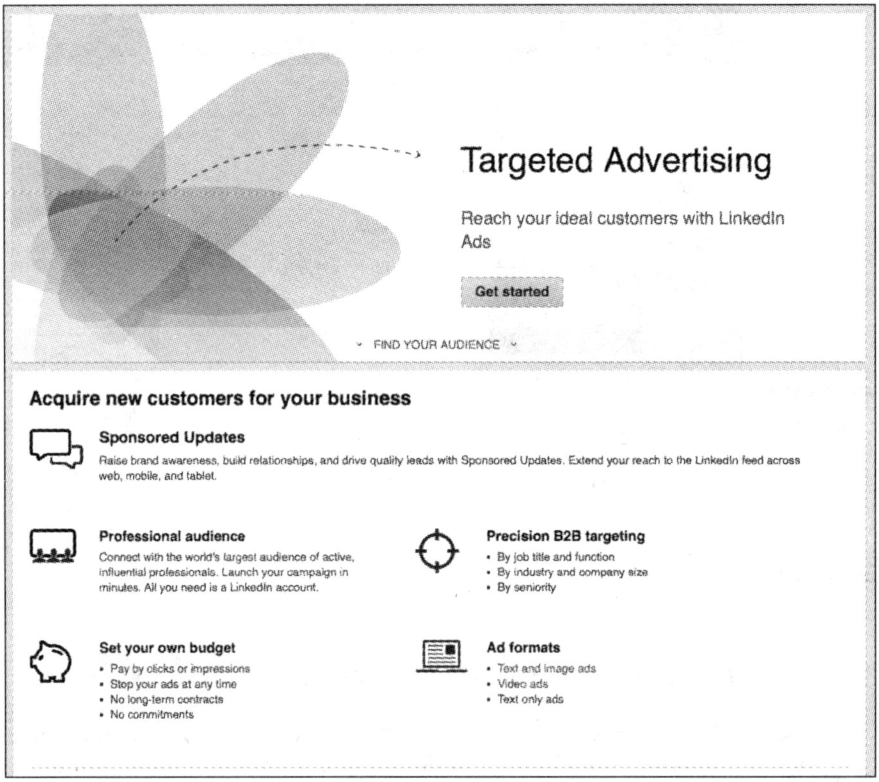

Figure 9-12: LinkedIn provides robust targeted advertising to reach subscribers.

Google+

Although it's not mentioned nearly as much as its rivals, Google+, as seen in Figure 9-13, quietly has become the second-largest social networking site in the world after Facebook. With more than 500 million active users, it's definitely a force to be reckoned with. Part of its appeal lies in its ability to interact with other Google properties such as Gmail and YouTube. You don't have to sign up for Google+ individually as long as you already have a Gmail account.

Although Google+ has numerous features and benefits, the ones that apply to your webinar needs are the ability to easily send e-mail invitations to Gmail users. But that also limits your scope. If you're reaching out to business professionals, be aware that not all of them will have a Gmail account.

Here are some helpful Google+ features to consider:

- **Communities:** Allow users to create ongoing conversations about particular topics.
- **Events:** Lets you add Events, invite people, and share photos and media in real time from the event. The program is integrated with Google Calendar and it has features similar to Facebook.
- **What's Hot:** A stream that shows which topics are commented on, interacted with, and shared the most on Google+. It's very similar to Twitter's trending topics.
- **Hangout:** Basically it's a free video conferencing call, as seen in Figure 9-14, that supports up to 10 people. You can share documents, a scratchpad, and screens with other users. In addition, built-in apps such as YouTube and Google Docs also work.

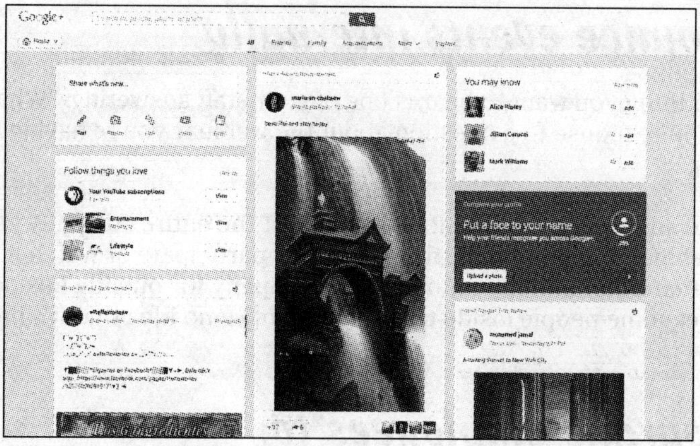

Figure 9-13: The very recognizable color and font of Google+.

Figure 9-14: A video chat with friends in the Google+ Hangout.

Utilizing Your Best Ambassadors: Your Employees

Although they usually don't wear exaggerated adornments on their garments and have likely never seen the interior of an embassy, your employees are the diplomats of your company. Don't overlook these vital resources when you're promoting your next webinar.

Regardless of the size of your company and what you're promoting, your employees provide exposure to many of the places overlooked by social media and e-mail invitations. Their word of mouth and Twitter skills may be just what the envoy ordered. The key is that you've got to communicate with them so they know what's going on.

Announce events internally

The last thing you want to hear is one of your staff answering: "What? We are? When?" in response to a question about the webinar you're having later that morning.

To avoid such embarrassment, be sure to let the entire company know about your webinar and encourage them to either participate or watch it on-demand later. Often a webinar is produced by a company for outside business contacts, yet some people inside the company have no idea that it's happening.

Encourage employees to tweet about events

Everyone from the mailroom to the boardroom should tweet about your next webinar. But will they? Not if you don't remind them. Remember, each occupation has its own set of similar followers, so just imagine the reach those tweets have to people you may have missed initially, especially if the webinar has broad appeal.

Ask sales to invite customers and prospects

TIP

Get your sales team to send invitations to their clients. After all, if anyone has great contact info, it's going to be this crew. Taking advantage here provides yet another avenue of potential participants and can also provide a bonding experience between the salesperson and the customer.

Create a webinar promotion timeline

REMEMBER

The early bird catches the worm, and the worm in this case refers to getting people interested in your webinar. Start early and keep the fire burning until the presenter says hello.

It's important that potential attendees know well in advance that a webinar is going to take place to give them time to consider. As the date draws near, send out more reminders over e-mail and social networking. The key is to first get them to register. The next few reminders should prod them to actually show up.

When to start

Send your e-mail invitation blast at least two weeks before the webinar. It's all right to send them earlier if you have something big planned and want to maximize exposure. You should rarely invite guests less than two weeks away. Of course, there are exceptions, but in order to get the most out of your invitation, you want to provide a solid two weeks of lead time. Follow up with a reminder one week before. Besides reminding them to register (if they did not already), this reiterates the objectives established on your landing page. It's a busy world, so it's not uncommon for someone to forget not only that they've registered for your webinar, but why they were compelled to do it in the first place.

When to stop

REMEMBER

Perhaps once upon a time there was a reason to stop sending letters before an event because they simply would not get there on time, but the days of Pony Express are gone. There's no reason to not send an e-mail reminder — even right before the event — because there's a chance someone who already registered will remember to log on, and some last-minute Jack can register and take part on the day of the webinar.

Send a reminder 24 hours before the event, and then two hours, and one hour before. You can even follow up with a 15-minute reminder to be on the safe side. E-mails sent right before the event often work best.

Demand an on-demand strategy

Just like you TiVo or DVR your favorite television shows, you can do the same when it comes to your webinar. This way, all of the people who couldn't make it for one reason or another have a chance to experience it. Make sure your provider offers a reliable on-demand strategy.

Distribute a link to registrants with on-demand content

Right after your webinar ends, send your audience a thank-you note for attending, and include a link for them to watch the webinar on demand. Here's a chance to get some of the folks who registered, but were not able to attend, to watch it. In addition, some of the people who experienced it may want to watch it again, or better yet, share it with a friend.

Here are just a few of the benefits of publicizing your on-demand link after the fact:

- Great way to reach registrants who couldn't attend
- Can increase your attendance by an average of 25 percent
- Significantly enhances event ROI (return on investment)

Part III
The Day of the Show

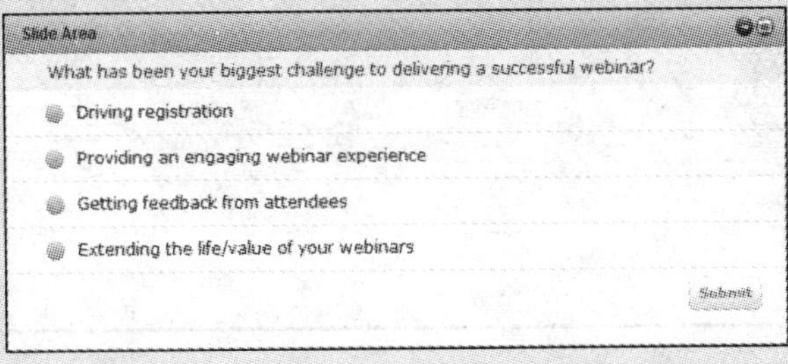

Visit www.dummies.com for tips on being a relevant webinar host.

In this part . . .

- Understand how to build Excel tables that hold and store the data you need to analyze.
- Find quick and easy ways to begin your analysis using simple statistics, sorting, and filtering.
- Get practical stratagems and commonsense tactics for grabbing data from extra sources.
- Discover tools for cleaning and organizing the raw data you want to analyze.

Chapter 10

Being the Presenter

In This Chapter

- Playing the part
- Wearing the right attire
- Preparing for the presentation
- Taking advantage of public speaking techniques

The presenter is the rock star of the webinar, usually without the leather pants and scarves. Not everyone can look and act like a rock star, and the same holds true for your presenter. And although your presenter may have fewer groupies than Justin Bieber (okay, probably none at all), he should be highly revered for his unique talent. Engaging groups of people numbering anywhere from fewer than a hundred to more than a thousand people across the world while being alone in a room with a computer takes a special talent.

So what does it take to be that special person who can be an effective webinar presenter?

Maybe you've done some presentations in the boardroom, spoken live to a small group, or addressed a larger audience at a local engagement. Perhaps you're a polished speaker who is comfortable behind a podium on a regular basis. Even if you've already presented at a webinar and are looking to improve your skills, you can learn something from this chapter.

Webinar presenters truly are a special breed, especially because they have to communicate to large audiences without the luxury of any affirmative feedback. (You know — the kind you get from looking your audience in the eye.) There's nothing like that immediate reaction from an audience right in front of you, but that luxury doesn't exist when presenting a webinar. Instead, the role seems to have more in common with being a radio disc jockey, without the benefit of music to make you more interesting to the audience.

The discussion that provides a smart perspective on "Understanding Analytics" or "Avoiding Social Media Faux Pas" is no less compelling than an hour of great music, but the presenter must possess some key qualities to successfully engage an audience. In this chapter, I show you some of them.

Looking the Part

As video becomes more widely used in webinars, the audience can actually see the presenter instead of just hearing a voice. That introduces another variable to the equation: the appearance of the speaker. The introduction of video into webinars is not quite as drastic as the move from radio programs to television shows, or silent films to the talkies, but it does nonetheless change the game.

But looking the part has much more to do than having flowing blonde locks, six-pack abs, or perhaps the more likely stereotype of a guy wearing khakis with a button-down shirt and a headset. Instead, looking the part is more about an attitude: having a presence in front of the camera that goes beyond what the eyes can see. It's about exuding confidence with every word and being sure that it comes through the technology. It's also about gaining trust. The participant must feel that you're an expert. When you add the perfect attire, a dose of swagger, and good body language, the successful presenter can look the part and effectively reach the audience on the other side of the connection.

Finding the best presenter for the job

Webinars can cover just about every topic under the sun, so depending on what the webinar is about, some presenters fit the role more convincingly than others. That's because the look of the presenter and cadence of her voice can play a big part in wowing the audience.

Here's an example scenario. If you were participating in a webinar called "The Ten Best Places to Retire in the U.S.," who would make you feel more comfortable: a charismatic retirement-aged presenter, or an equally charming kid just out of college? Regardless of her ability to speak convincingly to large groups, the relateability factor plays into the success of the presenter. In other words, an older audience wants to hear from someone near their own age on a retirement-related topic. And a business topic is presented more credibly by an adult wearing office attire.

Some factors to consider when choosing the right presenter include

- The industry being discussed
- The presentation format
- The content of the discussion
- The audience demographic

Dressing for the part

Unlike with movie stars, there's not much celebrity status that goes beyond the webinar for presenters (unless of course they are bona fide stars doing a webinar). A webinar doesn't have a red carpet where your presenters can pose and the press can ask them which designer's clothes they're wearing.

You still need to dress for the occasion, but there's no hard-and-fast rule that covers every circumstance. It's difficult to compare the webinar experience with the physical world where you adhere to some form of fashion convention. For example, it's not acceptable to go to a formal event like a wedding wearing flip-flops and a cut-off T-shirt. A dark suit would be a better choice, just as linen trousers are well suited for an evening pool party.

REMEMBER

Picking the correct wardrobe for a webinar is far more relaxed and often comes down to knowing your audience. You want to make sure that you're dressed appropriately for the presentation. Instead, you want them to pay attention to you. A hoodie might be fine for an audiocast, but it may not be the best choice when you are on video.

The presenter's attire needs to take into consideration a variety of factors that include the following suggestions:

TIP

- **Dress for the occasion:** The presenter's attire should reflect what the audience would wear. For example, if you're talking with an audience of students, dress casual. Conversely, if you're addressing a business audience, it's a good idea to wear what they wear, which more often than not is a suit. Of course, some audiences are hipper than others. If you're addressing a Silicon Valley audience, a suit is probably over-the-top.
- **Don't overdress (or underdress):** Wearing a three-piece suit for a webinar on an arts education topic may not convey the visual statement you're trying to make. The same holds true for speaking on-camera about capitalizing on the short sales market while wearing jeans and a T-shirt. It's better to dress like your audience.

- **Keep it simple:** If you're going to present on video, you need to adhere to certain rules. For example, it's not a good idea to wear white because you create a bright spot on the screen. Wearing complicated patterns can also cause a problem on video. For more on video, see Chapter 12.

Preparing for the Presentation

Having the right face for a particular audience or wearing the perfect clothes for the event can factor in the success of the presentation, but effective preparation techniques go well beyond the look of the speaker or how fashionable they appear. Instead, it's more important to master the content by fully understanding it and being able to deliver it clearly and concisely. That's going to matter most in the end because your web audience doesn't care that much about your fashion sense beyond that you dress somewhat like they do.

They only care that you're an expert on the topic and are equally proficient at making it easy for them to understand the subject matter. That's because familiarity with the topic is only half the battle. How you deliver it is equally as important, if not more so, and that comes from properly preparing for it. It's like you're rehearsing for a play. Yeah, you may know the lines to *Death of a Salesman* word for word, but that doesn't mean you can perform them without the proper preparation.

If you're not prepared for the conversation, your faults will come through quicker than a pair of canvas shoes gets wet in a downpour. And how will your audience respond to an erratic performance? Not very well, because they won't stick around for long. After all, it's easier to leave a webinar than to walk out of a packed hotel ballroom during a presentation.

Getting into your role as presenter

In addition to being a rock-star presenter, you also need to be a good Boy Scout and be prepared. Proper preparation relies on first making sure that the content is organized in a way that tells a compelling story. It's about more than just assembling the facts; it's about creating a flow. After you've done that, you must effectively present it.

Consider the following:

- **Build a narrative:** Take all the different parts of the story that you've assembled and put them together in a cohesive order. Create a comfortable segue that takes the audience on a journey that lets them know all the stops.

- **Compel your audience:** Support your words with reference images, video, and information graphics. When using slides with words on them, make sure they're not too text-heavy. Nobody likes to see that. You want to make sure that the slides are simply there to aid in the storytelling, not to tell the entire story themselves.
- **Prepare yourself:** Think of yourself as an athlete getting ready for a big game or an actor about to take the stage. Tell yourself that you're the storyteller, and your story is the presentation you're making. Essentially, you're the voice of reason and wonder, but you still have to have a strong visual presentation to aid in the telling of that story.

Practicing 'til you make perfect

TIP

Put aside your own feelings of how charismatic you are as a speaker, or how impressed you are with your own expertise on the subject matter, and instead concentrate on your performance. Remember: The key to a great presentation lies in practice. It's all about repetition. Read the presentation again and again before you get to the rehearsal phase so you can deliver the presentation fluidly. Besides, it's the only way to determine if you are running on time or need to edit your talking points. It also enables you to make adjustments for the right balance of slides and other visual assets in the presentation.

It's important for the presenter to remember that delivering a compelling presentation is not about speaking *at* people, but speaking *to* them. It's critical to understand you're having a conversation with a bunch of people on the other end of the line. And although, you may not be able to see them, you're standing right in front of them, so the more you're able to talk to them instead of at them, the more effective you will be.

Here are a few suggestions:

TIP

- **Come prepared:** Your other skills will mean very little if you don't show up prepared for the topic. An audience can sense when you're going through the motions. The second they pick up on it, they see the presentation as a waste of time and log off. Don't let that happen, especially because it's something totally under your control. Be prepared and focus on points that can help them and maybe even get them interacting later on.
- **Know your audience:** The more you know about the people you are addressing, the easier it is to communicate with them. Learn as much about them from the registration data as you can so you don't go over — or under — their heads. Using polls and surveys in the webinar also gives you an opportunity to assess the audience's experience and comprehension.

Moving and speaking

Don't underestimate the importance regarding your choice of words and body language. They play a big part in how you communicate to your audience. Of course, this partly applies to presentations where you're being captured on video, but it also refers to how you are heard by the audience.

Being aware of body language

How you move your body can sometimes communicate as much as what you say with your mouth. Unfortunately, we're mostly oblivious to what our hips are trying to say or what our hand gestures really mean. Regardless, the body acts as a strong communication tool that leads others to understand us a little better, but at times, can also muddy the waters. We've all heard of little traits that contradict the spoken word, such as a person touching his ear when he's asked a question (which can indicate lying), or looking away when asked a direct question (indicates not wishing to answer).

Regardless of whether we're aware of any of it, the audience can pick up on some gesture or motion and make assumptions about what it means. To avoid sending mixed signals and to understand your own body language, it's a good idea to examine some of the more oblivious gestures.

Remember, body language is not an exact science. These are just a set of guidelines to consider. Here are a few examples of what body language can say during your presentation. Don't just look at the list and assume these are all things to avoid; rather, check out what can work for dramatic effect:

- **Crossing the arms:** Unless it's really cold in the room, this could mean the speaker is either reserved or trying to cover their self-consciousness.
- **Hands on hips:** This gesture can be construed as an aggressive call for action, or a sign of waiting or impatience.
- **Clinched fist:** This is a sign of irritation, nervousness, or anger, or could refer to a call for action.
- **Direct eye contact:** True, you're looking into the camera, but viewers feel that you're looking into their eyes. When you look someone directly in the eye, you're establishing trust and truthfulness. Conversely, when you look away as you say something, it can mean you're either not convinced of what you're saying or not telling the truth.
- **Tilted head:** Maybe the speaker is a Labrador Retriever that just heard an unfamiliar word. If it's an actual human, however, a tilted head combined with a smile can indicate playfulness. Combined with a raised eyebrow, it can mean a challenge. If the speaker also has a slightly open mouth, a tilted head can express confusion.

Considering Presentation Techniques

That cliché of not getting a second chance to make a first impression holds a great deal of truth, especially when you make a presentation over the Internet to people you cannot see. Getting an audience to like you is hard enough, but when you're not in the same room with them, it's hard to measure your performance. That doesn't make it any less important.

That's why being comfortable with the material and being sincere go a long way. Whenever an audience feels that they can learn something from you, they tend to stick around. You can liven things up a little by injecting a little humor, you know, like making exaggerated analogies. But remember, that's not the same as trying to add a punchline. Unless you're a professional comedian, don't try too hard to be funny.

There's a golden rule about performing in front of large groups from every person who has ever spoken in a room filled with people, and that's "Don't try to be funny." That's because very few people are actually funny. So trying to transform yourself into a comedian ends up looking fake, and that's not an endearing quality for a webinar presenter. Instead, concern yourself with how you effectively tell a story.

You can appeal to your audience in a way that engages them, too.

Consider the following:

- **Know the subject matter:** I can't overstate how important it is for the audience to regard the speaker as an expert.
- **Use humor:** Don't try to make jokes. Instead, take a light approach to explaining some of your topics. It could be as subtle as poking fun at the sound of a particular word or even making fun of your own experiences. Audiences relate well to that because it makes them feel like you're like them. Just don't make fun of the audience. No one likes that.
- **Ask rhetorical questions:** Peppering your speech with occasional rhetorical questions has been proven to help listeners retain information they heard. Questions stimulate the participant's brain. Studies show that audiences remember less about what you say and more about the questions that you ask.
- **Be rhythmic:** Repeat the key points of the presentation so they sink in. Remember: People tend to absorb information through repetition.
- **Use analogies:** Explaining complex ideas using common comparisons makes it much easier for an audience to understand a complicated topic. Compare complex issues to something simpler and more relatable when you can.

Driving Engagement

When it comes to engaging the audience, the presenter sits in the driver's seat. Whether it's a single voice presenting, or a team of speakers, everyone involved has the same goal: to keep the audience interested. Every aspect of the presentation needs to work in unison. Slides, graphics, and video all are there to assist the speaker in telling the particular story of the webinar. It's essential that the participant remains engaged from start to finish, and then even after that by following up, but it's the presenter who steers the audience through the racecourse.

- **Utilize the tools provided by the webinar platform to increase engagement:** The best way to increase engagement is to provide opportunities for interaction, such as Q&As, chat, social media integration, and polls and surveys.
- **Be personable:** You must be able to connect with the audience. The more you're able to effectively connect with people who are not in front of you, the more you can engage them. Projecting an engaging personality is an art form that not everyone can master, however.
- **Establish trust:** People have to buy into you as an expert or as a trusted advisor. If you can establish trustworthiness, you've relaxed your audience for the journey.
- **Don't read to them:** Nothing creates a barrier between you and the audience like reading from a cue card or piece of paper. Audiences see it and it hinders the connection between you and them. Don't read your slides, either.
- **Take a breath and pause:** Just because the webinar is on a strict schedule doesn't mean you have to speed-talk your way through the presentation. It's a good idea to take a breath and pause. This provides the audience some time to process the information.
- **Entertain them:** That doesn't mean you should belt out a tune or crack jokes. (*Please*, don't sing or crack jokes.) Instead, try to understand how they perceive the topic and appeal to their emotions through wonder and mild humor.
- **Give them something that makes their situation better:** This is perhaps the most important means of engaging your audience. If you can easily explain how something makes their life better, you have them in the palm of your hand.

Chapter 11

Engaging with the Audience

In This Chapter

- Building engagement with the audience
- Soliciting feedback from your participants
- Working with your production team
- Clearing up lingering questions

Thanks to technology, the rules of engagement have changed so much that it's no longer necessary for a speaker to be in the same room with an audience to find a way to "connect" with them.

Ten years ago, if someone proposed the idea that you could engage an audience with words and pictures from behind a screen, you might think they were talking about being on television news, or better yet, wonder if they'd recently watched *The Wizard of Oz.*

The great and all-powerful Oz was able to control and communicate without ever being seen. Of course, he was a fraud, but the point remains the same: It's possible to reach people without being seen.

As the webinar grows as a powerful tool for reaching a mass audience, a similar eerie isolation takes place behind the scenes. Addressing large audiences, a speaker — sometimes alone in a room — attempts to connect with people all over the planet through their computer screens and mobile devices.

Although there are no witches (good or bad) or flying monkeys patrolling the airwaves, a lot of things can still go wrong, thereby causing people to lose interest. That makes the onus of engaging the audience the major task for the webinar producer.

But audience engagement seems like such a tall order, especially with the audience being so disconnected from the process. That's why audience engagement is "job one" when it comes to webinar success. Engaging the throngs of people that you cannot see requires a multilayered approach centered on both the interaction tools and the personality of the presenter.

Building Engagement in the Presentation

Engage your audience, don't enrage them. (Actually, come to think of it, enraging them would probably still be better than simply boring them with a humdrum discussion and wordy slides.)

Do you want to know the secret to engaging your audience? It lies in the interactivity of the presentation. That's where the audience feels like they're an important part of the process. There's a concerted effort to move away from the day when webinars were in broadcast mode to webinars that enable a real conversation with the audience. That conversation is where most of the real engagement takes place during the event.

Making the most of social sharing tools

Social sharing tools provide valuable information on how your audience feels about the presentation. In addition, they allow users to share the event with their peers. Social media has become such a part of the webinar experience that companies are integrating Twitter, LinkedIn, and Facebook directly into the webinar experience. That's because people want to react to the content and share their reactions in real time.

That's why it's important that social media tools are built directly into your webinar console. You don't want audience members leaving every time they feel compelled to comment, so having a Twitter feed right in the console keeps them from straying. The next time the participant hears something that inspires them and they want to tweet about it, they can do it right there as a part of the webinar. It becomes a social conversation that takes place, especially if you have a predetermined hashtag for your webinar for Twitter.

Besides social media, there are other tools that let the rubber hit the road, so you're able to have multidirectional conversation.

These include

TIP

- **Polling:** The presenters can poll the audience, as seen in Figure 11-1, and then comment on the results, perhaps building a discussion around it. This brings the voice of the audience into the presentation.
- **Live Q&A:** Whether you have the question-and-answer session at the end, or maybe interspersed throughout the presentation, letting audience members submit questions directly to the presenters, as seen in Figure 11-2, engages them on several levels. The presenter can answer each question, bringing the voice of the audience into the conversation. Remember, real-time interaction keeps people engaged.

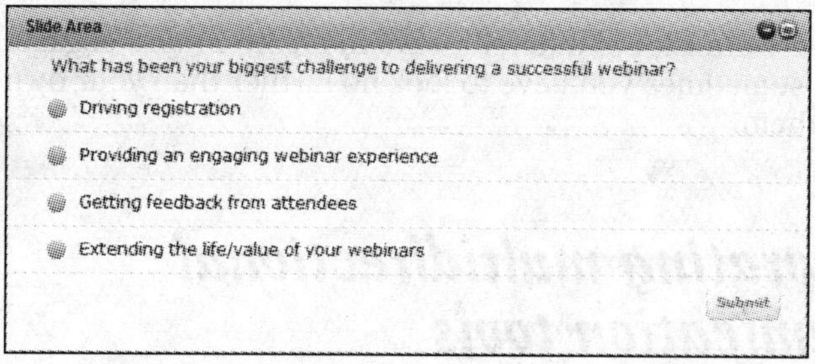

Figure 11-1: A sample poll.

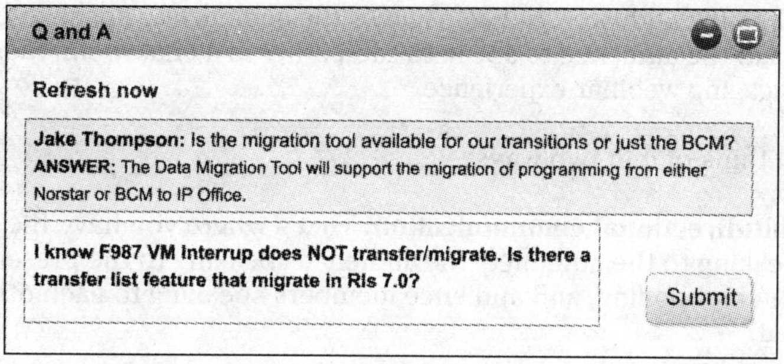

Figure 11-2: A Q&A console.

Using collaboration tools

Basically *collaboration tools* can be anything and everything that help people communicate with each other. In the analog world, it could be as simple as passing a pad and pen from person to person in a small group. You could also refer to a conference call over phone lines as a collaboration tool. It doesn't matter as long as it works in getting the group to share information.

Webinars use their own unique brand of group collaboration and communication tools. Although they are similar to one another, they are also slightly different.

Group collaboration tools provide the means for people to submit ideas, vote on them, rank them, or collaborate on those ideas as the webinar is going on. This can be done for training webinars and learning sessions, but it can also be done for general topics or conversations.

Group communication tools deal with chat and social media. Participants can tweet about the presentation to an external audience, or post comments on Facebook. You can have a live chat between participants going on during the webinar, as if your audience members were "talking" to each other.

Although there are a lot of different ways to create a more engaging webinar experience, sometimes you have to look no further than your own audience and dazzle them.

Incorporating multidirectional communication tools

A *multidirectional communication tool* is one that allows not only the presenter to speak to the audience, but also allows the audience to speak to the presenter, and the audience to speak to each other in a chat room, thus creating a more engaging webinar experience.

You can think of it in two ways:

- **Multidirectional communication:** That's where you have the presenter speaking to the audience, the audience speaking to the presenter via Q&A and polling, and audience members speaking to each other using chat.
- **Collaboration:** The tools that produce the high levels of interactivity. Everything from the note you passed to the girl in front of you in grade school to the various forms of social media, online communication, and video helps individuals reach one another and can produce a more engaging experience in the webinar.

Dazzle them with moving pictures

Video continually gains ground as the emerging star of the webinar circuit. It's becoming a great way to personalize your presentation along with being an effective tool for engaging the audience. Research shows that when you integrate video, participant attention and focus increase, making webinar viewing times last a little bit longer.

Earlier in the millennium, the average time spent looking at an online video was just over a minute. The prominence of YouTube extended the viewing time to a few minutes, and now that the disrupters — Hulu, Netflix, and Amazon Prime — base their business models on online long-form video, users will watch an online video for a much longer span than they used to.

So consider either using video for your next presentation, or expand what you're already doing with it.

You can use video in your webinar in a variety of ways. These include

- **Integrating video clips into a presentation:** Anything from a short promo to a viral video will work. Sometimes the video supports the topic, whereas other times, you can show it on its own.
- **Having your presenters presenting on video or webcams:** These days, many webinars already include a video feed of the presenter, but not all of them do. If you're not showing your presenter, consider doing it for you next webinar — it can prove to be an effective tool.
- **Broadcasting live from a studio or other event:** It's not unusual for a presentation to include a live feed of a speaker at the local convention center, a television-style interview session, or a highly produced moderated panel. It all works out because live video provides another way to engage your audience. See Chapter 12 for more information.

Methods for Fielding Feedback

Like echolocation to a bat finding his way around without a handy pair of spectacles, feedback is an equally important tool for the webinar producer. Not only does it serve as a means of determining what you're doing right — and what you're doing wrong — but it also lets you know what your viewing audience clamors to see. And when you understand their needs as a whole, you can cater to them. You naturally increase engagement because they feel like part of the process.

Collecting feedback is an important step in the evolution of your webinar, so take advantage of the opportunity to do it before, during, and after the webinar.

You can start looking for feedback before you even hold the webinar. Of course, the results will be premature, but such feedback still has its place. Although it's not often used, a pre-engagement feedback blitz makes it possible to stimulate an audience before you actually hold the event. It differs from a survey, which is taken at the end of the webinar.

Lots of producers rely on pre-event surveys that they put on registration and landing pages to solicit content or to find out what people's expectations are before the event. These include potential questions as well as their expectations for the session. Think of it as the buildup before the big game.

But more effectively, the feedback process takes place during and certainly after the webinar. From there, you can compile enough information and data to gauge its success.

Let me break down feedback technique at each stage:

- **Before the webinar:** You can have a pre-event survey that uses questions such as, "What would you like to learn from this event?" Or "What three categories are most interesting to you?" Basically, when you survey your registered audience to see what they are interested in — or maybe just ask for information from them beyond your gated form — it's an opportunity to collect information from them in addition to what you can learn from the registration process.
- **During the presentation:** As the webinar takes place, you're collecting information in a number of different ways. First, you've got poll results, which provide information on the fly. Next, there's a Q&A session with all the questions that are submitted. Collecting information on both is essential. Then you have the ability to look at all the other interactive tools and how they are performing. For example, you could look at what people are saying in chat rooms and on social media forums.
- **Afterward:** The post-event survey provides direct feedback on the presentation as a whole, including the host's performance. That survey, as seen in Figure 11-3, is automatically generated to the audience at the end of the presentation. Some push it to the audience in real time, whereas others provide buttons that participants can click to fill out the survey (but you need to encourage people to do that). The information is delivered directly through the webinar tool to the audience. You can also collect additional information from the Twitter hashtag you assigned to the event. Social media provides a whole new way of getting post-event feedback by seeing what people are saying online. Platform providers now offer benchmark indices and engagement scores that make webinar analytics "actionable," with performance comparisons with other webinars.

Figure 11-3: A sample post-webinar survey.

Working with a Moderator

Wearing many hats, the moderator plays a big part when it comes to maintaining audience engagement through a steady and consistent flow. Typically the moderator is the first voice you hear at the webinar, setting the stage by introducing the console, discussing the housekeeping, and introducing the speaker and topics.

REMEMBER

Flow plays a big role in engaging the audience because it keeps everything moving at a nice pace, so consider the moderator a key in the audience engagement machine. By maintaining order, keeping the speakers on track, and making sure the audience is fully aware of all that's going on within the presentation, the journey itself adds to the engagement of all those that attend.

Here is a summary of what the moderator does to engage the audience:

- Introduce the presentation
- Make sure everything runs on time
- Keep the audience in the loop
- Deal with the Q&A
- Thank the audience for attending

Do you know what doesn't engage the audience? If this were a game show and you answered "Having a bad speaker," you'd more than likely win the washer/dryer combination behind door number one. Not having a good presenter is a definite webinar killer. All the fun engagement tools in the world can't overcome a bad speaker. People are too busy to patiently listen to someone who isn't giving them what they need from the discussion.

You don't need Tony Robbins delivering your presentation, but you do need a compelling speaker at the podium. Make sure that you're using great speakers even if they are not content experts. You may have experts who know more about the subject matter than anybody else, but they also may not be comfortable being an online speaker. Instead of taking a chance, you can develop the content for the webinar and have a qualified speaker present it. Think of it as writing a song, and letting a better singer perform it. Then, you can always bring those experts back in for a Q&A. Some folks are just boring or very uncomfortable in front of an audience, so you want to be really careful about putting them in front of a microphone.

The speaker should have some of these qualities:

- **Shows passion about the topic:** When the speaker really understands the subject matter and feels strongly about it, it comes through to the audience.
- **Talks to the audience, not at it:** The importance of this cannot be overstated. Do you want a webinar presentation to sound like a lecture from your seventh-grade science teacher or like a conversation with a colleague you're commuting with on the train?
- **Understands the audience's attention span:** All human beings have a short attention span, and really busy people have an even shorter one. Keep the topic moving.

Leaving No Question Unanswered

The policy of a successful presentation should be that no question is ever left behind. That's easier said than done because a webinar is usually fairly short, and a really large one with lots of interested parties can draw far more questions than can be answered in the entire webinar, never mind the allocated Q&A period.

In a truly successful webinar, you're going to get more questions than you can answer online. You are soliciting information in a number of ways. You may be getting questions via a Q&A widget. You may be getting data from polls. In some cases, people tweet questions. Regardless of how they ask, or when you answer, it is essential to make sure that every single question gets answered.

Consider the following:

- **Have a longer Q&A window:** If you anticipate the content will generate more questions than usual, consider adding a few minutes to the typical Q&A period.
- **Assemble a team of answer specialists:** Not all questions can be answered in the Q&A part of the presentation, but that's not to say you can't have members of your team answering questions via social media or e-mail.
- **Answer questions post-webinar:** If a question is not answered on-air, it must be answered off-air as quickly as possible. That means sending it directly to the customer via e-mail. The good news is that getting those questions answered creates opportunity to extend the conversation.
- **Accept questions during on-demand replay:** What? Yes. Even when your live event is over and you're offering it on demand, you can still accept questions. It's a really valid process for on-demand webinars. The only difference is that viewers don't get the questions answered on the air in real-time. Here's how it works: They submit a question and you have a process where those questions either get sent to somebody or put in a queue. Then they're automatically shuffled to an expert who will call them or provide them with an answer in whatever format you see fit. There should always be a process built-in to make sure every single question gets answered.

Chapter 12

Lights, Camera, Action . . .

In This Chapter

- Adding video to your presentation
- Getting by with a webcam
- Understanding your equipment needs
- Producing a multi-camera setup

Even before the 1902 silent film *A Trip to the Moon*, the moving picture was becoming an important tool for all kinds of expression. Now it's become something that we can't live without. Can you imagine watching a baseball game with just audio play-by-play and a bunch of information slides? Not cool.

Televising a live-action game certainly makes it more fun to watch. Similarly, it's a no-brainer to add video to your webinar: It transforms the event from a radio-like program to a television show.

For the past couple of years, video has slowly crept its way into the webinar experience, with many producers opting to put their presenter in front of the camera, or at the very least, integrating video clips into the presentation, sometimes even through PowerPoint.

That drives engagement through the roof, and people stick around for much longer to watch your presentation.

Maybe you want to alert Mr. DeMille (Cecil B., that is) that you're ready for your close-up. Or perhaps you simply want to see how well your next presentation works with video. One thing remains certain — using the moving picture as a key component for your webinar is a development that's here to stay.

Knowing What You Want

Whenever video is incorporated into a presentation, something magical happens. Communication and interest become greatly enhanced for obvious reasons. Being able to watch the presenter's facial expression, observe their body language, and look into their eyes (okay, via a screen, but it still counts) help viewers feel as though they know the presenter. This familiarity often motivates them to watch for longer periods. It's as if the viewers can look directly into the presenter's eyes, so they feel the presenter is in the same room with them.

If the presenter is sincere, the audience feels a bond with him, and will more likely trust what's being said. This connection makes the whole discussion more sincere while establishing credibility for your product or service. It's almost like the attendees are watching television, only the content informs them in a more specific manner.

Take the webinar out of your comfort zone

Once upon a time, movies were silent, television sets emitted a really bad-looking picture, as seen in Figure 12-1, and webinars were sound-driven graphic presentations. Video has changed the webinar experience to something closely resembling a television show, and with better quality than we had in the days of small screens and rabbit ears.

Besides having the talent on camera, you can also integrate video clips to counteract stodgy slides and still images. And the fun doesn't stop there. Slightly alter the format and have the presenter interview one or more experts to recreate the feel of a TV talk show. What about taking your ambition a step further by producing a multi-camera moderated panel of guests reminiscent of those televised Sunday morning political debate shows? All of that is possible when you introduce video into the webinar equation.

Figure 12-1: A simulation of a 1960s television image.

Be aware of the downside

Television production takes much more planning and resources to get it right; otherwise, it can look amateurish. Part of that responsibility is knowing who has great camera presence and who does not. Quite simply, sometimes the talent (your speakers and presenters) is just not right for video for one reason or another. Not every speaker is comfortable addressing the camera.

A classic example of the power of television brings to mind the first televised presidential debate during the 1960 election between Richard Nixon and John F. Kennedy. On television, Nixon appeared pale, tired, and sweaty, whereas Kennedy seemed relaxed, tanned, and vibrant.

Interestingly enough, television viewers claim Kennedy won the debate, whereas radio listeners gave the nod to Nixon. They felt he was more articulate and easier to understand compared to Kennedy with his thick New England accent.

Many claim that televised debate cost Nixon the presidency in that very close election. Regardless of the validity of this claim, it's clear that video can influence viewer perception. For that reason, you need to make sure that your speaker is comfortable and charismatic on camera.

The benefits of using video in your webinar

It's always better to look at a moving image. It's also human nature to trust someone you can both see and hear, rather than just hear. Even if the talking head is on someone's computer screen, people can identify with someone they can see.

The speaker's knowledge of the subject matter obviously plays a big role in the effectiveness of the presentation, but physical appearance and likability also factor into the equation. Making sure that you have the right people to put on-camera is certainly a factor, but the effort involved in that search seems like a small price to pay to take your webinar to the next level.

Here's why video works in your presentation:

- **Your audience can see the speaker:** The audience gets to see a real person as opposed to just hearing a voice. That's because speaking alone doesn't fully communicate your message to an audience. When you add body language, facial expressions, and other gestures, you've upped your game because all of those things factor into helping the audience understand your message.

- **You can use video clips:** Besides showing the presenter, you can also integrate your promotional video clips, video segments, and YouTube clips, as seen in Figure 12-2, into your presentation.
- **It takes your webinar into the modern age:** Video lets the presenter veer closer to what the audience is used to seeing; namely, a televised image. Audiences are always more receptive to the moving image.

And if that's not enough, here are some eye-opening statistics about video:

- According to the Internet analytics site ComScore, 89 million people in the United States will watch 1.2 billion online videos in a single day.
- A survey by Kantar Media states that only about 26 percent of national brands are using online video to market to consumers.
- Social Media Examiner says 76 percent of marketers plan to add video to their sites, making it a higher priority than Facebook, Twitter, and blog integration.

Figure 12-2: YouTube clips to which you have rights can make a great addition to your presentation.

So many ways to use video, so little time

Your webinar broadcast can either have the simple look and feel of a video blog or the complex production associated with a television show. How you plan to use video for your next presentation depends on what you're trying to accomplish, not to mention your budget.

It's always a good to use less. Don't use a bazooka to kill a mouse. Instead, you should always use video in the simplest form that your presentation requires. In other words, don't think you need a broadcast camera plunked down in front of the presenter sitting at a desk addressing 87 participants. Conversely, if you have a moderated panel of speakers and expect thousands of attendees to tune in, obviously your video needs will be greater.

Here are a few ways to use video:

- **Single camera:** Whether it's a webcam or large camcorder, this static shot positions the camera somewhere in front of the presenter.
- **Multiple presenters:** The medley of faces and voices sends multi-layered message, providing the audience with a better sense of the conversation. Sometimes each speaker sits in the same seat for her turn in front of a webcam or other camera. Other times, the speakers are in different places, requiring more than one camera.
- **Interview-style:** It's helpful for the audience to see both the presenter asking the questions and the guest answering. It's also beneficial to see facial expressions and body language. This is done either by panning the camera between speakers or using a two-camera setup.
- **Moderated panel:** Can you imagine how confusing it would be to listen to three speakers and a host yammering on without seeing who's saying what? For that reason, video is essential with this format.

Wearing the Director's Hat

I'm not referring to a French beret, unless of course, that's your thing. Instead, I'm talking about the need for another person on the team. Although video makes the webinar seem more personal, it also takes some effort to pull it off. Often the producer takes on the role of television director, especially with smaller presentations. More expansive productions generally dedicate a director to deal with the video-related issues. Some more ambitious shoots require a full television crew.

A single speaker hosting a small-scale webinar shares more in common with a radio disc jockey than a television host, with the exception of the static video shot. For many situations, it's perfectly acceptable to use a simple camera setup, or even a webcam. But as your webinar plan expands, before long, you can have a setup that rivals your favorite talk show.

Webcam

Once upon a time, the webcam was a cool accessory for your computer that let you visually communicate with your friends and family. It produced a relatively low-quality image, but was still pretty amazing for its time. As technology has improved, a built-in webcam now comes standard on many laptops and computers. The quality has gotten so much better that it's no longer evident that you're on a webcam.

Webcams are sufficient for many types of presentations, just as long as the presenter sits in front of the camera. This works well with smaller to medium-sized webinars, making the source of video a non-issue. Lighting, on the other hand, is another story. More on that later in this chapter in the section "Having the Right Equipment."

Single-camera shoot

A single-camera shoot can refer to anything that's not a webcam — built-in or otherwise — including anything from an inexpensive camcorder or GoPro (a small, inexpensive, high-definition video camera that you can stick just about anywhere) up to a DSLR (digital single-lens reflex) or broadcast-quality model. Regardless of which end of the spectrum you choose, the camera requires an operator and must be mounted to a tripod placed in front of the speaker. These models offer superior image quality and control compared to a webcam, but they also require a bit more finesse to make sure nothing goes wrong.

Multiple-camera shoot

Multiple-camera shoots should be reserved for larger, more sophisticated presentations. Multiple-camera shoots share many things in common with television production, so you need an expert team to manage these situations. Not only do you need someone to stand behind each camera and work their magic, but if you're going out live, the shoot also requires a technical director behind the scenes looking at the output of the various camera feeds and continuously switching them for the signal going out to the viewer. This setup works well with a moderated panel, but can also be used for a larger interview-style presentation.

TIP

Another option is to record studio videos. They are inserted in a live webinar and seem live, which is called *simu-live*.

A technical director

Have you ever wondered why football looks so great on television? The average regular season game uses at least ten cameras, and it's the job of the technical director to take all of those shots and angle and transform them into a logical arrangement where the most important shot from a particular camera is on-screen at the right moment.

For example, in a football game, as seen in Figure 12-3, Camera 1 would show the wide shot of the field; Camera 2, the snap of the ball; Camera 3, the quarterback set to pass in the pocket; and Camera 4, the receiver catching the ball. That's a bit oversimplified, but that's the basic job of a video switcher, as seen in Figure 12-4, and the technical director.

Although it's nowhere near as complicated, that same process happens during a webinar presentation, where the technical director, or TD, as he is commonly called, decides what each camera should shoot, and switches it to the output screen so what you see looks like an edited version.

Figure 12-3: Football on television would be hard to follow if not for the sophisticated technique of switching between multiple cameras.

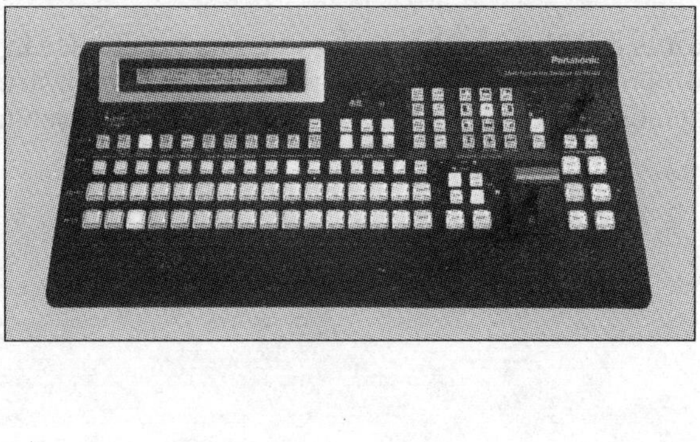

Figure 12-4: A video control room console with switcher.

Multiple locations

It's a pretty cool feeling when you're the presenter and you tell the audiences that this next speaker is coming to you live from the local convention center. Some webinars will use remote locations for a speaker. This is a more sophisticated version of using of the multiple-camera setup. Although large-scale events with huge budgets may opt for a broadcast transmission, more often these days it's done using some form of IP streaming. It's a bit more complex than producing the webinar, however, especially if you have never done it before.

It requires much more coordination and equipment. If that's what you need to do, be sure that either your webinar provider has the means to accomplish this task, or hire a production company that can do it.

Putting a studio over your head

When you've got a big production in the works, the question of "Why not use the conference room?" is simply answered: quality!

The capabilities provided by a professional studio will generate (ROI) Return On Investment for your brand in the form of a higher-quality finished product.

Face it, the reward for a sophisticated video-driven webcast is increased exposure, awareness, and confidence. So in a controlled environment focused on one thing: producing high quality video. The studio allows your speakers to focus on content and not worry about the technical setup, as seen in Figure 12-5. In addition, a studio is a comfortable environment for speakers, helping to get the best performances out of everyone on camera.

If you shop around, you can cut down on costs without sacrificing the quality of the production. For example, look for a studio that has built-in set options, because 15% of cost goes to labor and materials associated with setup and teardown of a given production. So if the set is already there, that's money you won't have to spend.

Another key factor is making sure that the studio has experience in live events, along with a control room for managing the presentation, and a strong Internet connection. Remember, there are no second takes when your webinar is live.

When deciding on a studio, consider the following:

- Built-in set pieces and a common backdrop for webinar productions.
- Adaptable elements that help your production appear "on-brand," such as colored lighting.
- Enough resources (cameras, lights, microphones, and so on) to support the full scope of your event.
- Green screen systems that allow you to superimpose a unique background for the presenter.

Figure 12-5: A live webinar with video crew behind the scenes.

Making Your Studio Webcast Work

Studio scenarios work great for both live and on-demand webcasts. While the success of the production depends on careful pre-production preparation and the right studio facility, that doesn't always guarantee success. You have to look no further than what is on television. Some shows works well, others not so much.

Take a look at television news programs and the formats that work for them. Some have a news anchor behind a desk, while others offer a slightly more "comfortable" setting. Regardless, the key is to create a real dialog about the issue at hand. This approach requires careful attention to the content but can deliver great results.

Here's some ways to do it:

- Ask speakers to provide the talking points they wish to address
- Frame questions that match your host's talking points/key messages
- Have a roundtable discussion in the studio
- Edit the discussion down to a usable segment length and create an accompanying slide presentation
- Release the discussion as a simulated live broadcast

The "right" format is simply one that's easily accessible for your particular audience. See Chapter 5 for more information. But also be aware of some formats, or settings that don't work.

- **Anything overly scripted:** Not only does it lack spontaneity, but comes off as "canned."
- **The lecture:** Face it, nobody likes being lectured, and when your audience can easily slip out and log onto Netflix, it's something you should avoid.
- **Contrived sets:** Unless you're watching *Pee-wee's Playhouse,* leave the big comfy chairs and fireside chats in the rear view mirror.

Having the Right Equipment

Anyone who has ever been a professional photographer or at least a serious hobbyist knows that a camera is merely the tip of the iceberg when it comes to equipment. You need all sorts of accessories to make it work. The same holds true for video gear for your webinar. A video camera on its own can't do much, unless of course your goal is dark, shaky video clips.

Here I take a look at everything you need to integrate video into your next presentation, from the most basic piece of equipment to the most sophisticated.

Video camcorder

The most obvious piece of equipment, the video camcorder takes on many forms, from built-in webcam, as seen in Figure 12-6, to a high-end studio camera. And depending on the scale of the presentation, probably somewhere in between lies the right match for your needs.

Figure 12-6: A built-in webcam on Apple iMac all-in-one desktop computer.

Microphone

Just about every recording device that most of us own today includes a microphone, but not all can provide the pristine audio quality that you'll require for the audience to clearly understand what you have to say.

Although a built-in microphone pales in comparison to using a separate microphone, it's not always possible when using a webcam (because it may not support an auxiliary cable). Whether you're looking to capture the sound of a group by using a *shotgun* microphone, a *stick* mic for conducting a stand-up interview, or a microphone clipped to the lapel of the speaker, there are clear advantages to using a separate microphone held away from the camera.

Here are some choices:

- **Lavaliere:** It's the clip-on microphone often associated with television interviews, as seen in Figure 12-7. Also called a *lapel mic*, it attaches to the subjects' clothing about six to nine inches from the mouth.
- **Stick microphone:** Used for a variety of situations ranging from speaking on a stage to conducting a stand-up interview, as seen in Figure 12-8.

  Shotgun microphone: Mounted on a stand or on a pole with a technician holding it over the speaker, this type of microphone can pick up sound from longer distances. It works well with a moderated panel or interview format.

Figure 12-7: The lavaliere microphone is almost undetectable, yet it picks up a clear audio signal.

Figure 12-8: The hand-held microphone works well but must be positioned close to the subject.

Audio mixer

It's the cool-looking console in a recording studio with all the sliders, as seen in Figure 12-9. Of course, you don't need anything that sophisticated. But when you're combining sound from multiple sources into a single channel or signal, it's necessary to use a mixer. In addition to altering sound levels, the audio board lets you tweak the signals' level, frequency content, and dynamics to refine the sound quality. Although many webinar situations can simply do without an audio mixer, whenever you introduce two or more audio sources, using one is a good idea.

Figure 12-9: A Mackie 8-channel audio mixer.

Your three-legged friend, the tripod

The tripod is your three-legged friend for many reasons, with the most obvious being that it allows you to keep the camera steady. They come in a variety of sizes and types and are constructed of various materials, as seen in Figure 12-10. They all do the same thing, and yet each has its own purpose in specific situations.

Consider the criteria for finding the best one for your needs:

- **Price:** With a range in price from very affordable to ultra-expensive, most tripods do the same job, but vary when it comes to size and durability. Sturdy models on the affordable side tend to be relatively heavier than their more expensive counterparts.
- **Materials:** The cost of a tripod goes up as the weight goes down. An aluminum model costing around $100 suddenly costs $500 when it's made of the more durable and lighter metal alloys like carbon fiber.
- **Size:** Moviemaking requires a tripod with a height that at least meets your eye level; otherwise, it's not going to be comfortable to use.
- **Controls:** It sounds trite, but the controls for extending your tripod play a big part in its ease of use. Some lock by turning; others use clips or control knobs. When you can, pick a model with controls that change quickly and seem intuitive to you.
- **Separate pieces:** Less expensive tripods are usually sold as a whole unit with legs and a head, whereas more sophisticated models are purchased separately. Affordable video tripods work well with DSLRs, but if you feel your needs warrant it, buy the legs and head that suit your needs.

Figure 12-10: A standard video tripod with fluid head.

Lighting

Video quality is only as good as the lighting on the scene. To look our best, humans require soft, directional illumination. Unfortunately, the only way this can happen in an office situation is if you were to lie on your back looking up while conducting your webinar. Avant-garde shoots aside, that's not a very good idea. Then again, neither is trying to figure out how to use a sophisticated lighting kit if you have no experience. But don't fret — there are some simple solutions:

- **An on-camera light:** If you're using a video camera on a tripod, you can purchase this accessory that mounts atop the camera. The illumination is less than perfect, but with the proper diffusion (a filter or paper material to soften the light), it can work.
- **A portable soft box:** A better solution is to use a portable *soft box*, as seen in Figure 12-11, to provide nice, even illumination. Basically, the box attaches over the light source. You can find them at your favorite camera store for around a hundred bucks.
- **Large shaded lamp:** You can mimic the soft box look by using a translucent lampshade on your desk out of camera range.

Figure 12-11: A portable soft box.

Lighting kits

When your needs are more ambitious, you can bring your own lighting kit to exercise proactive control at the scene. Light kits range in price from a few hundred to a few thousand dollars. You can also buy them used for significantly less money.

Here's a list of the components in the case and the role they play:

- **Light head:** Using either a quartz lamp or LEDs, these high-output lights provide up to 1,000 watts of power or more.
- **Barn doors:** This standard accessory attaches to the front of the light and uses four hinged metal doors to shape its beam as well as preventing the distinctive scatter of light.
- **Stand:** Stands support the head and allow you to position the light at various angles and heights. Varying in size, they go from short and stout to quite high.

- **Umbrella:** You can soften illumination from the light head by turning it away from the subject and bouncing into a reflective umbrella. This softens and diffuses the light and produces a flattering illumination for the subject. Umbrellas come in various sizes and reflective surfaces.
- **Soft box:** A soft box is a large box-like enclosure that goes over the light head. The light reflects off the interior surface and it comes through the diffusing material at the front of the box, creating a soft, even illumination.

Match the Light to Your Situation

Understanding lighting concepts is a start, but making sure that the lighting works for your situation is what really matters.

Consider the following:

- **Understand the nature of the light source:** Some light sources offer a very narrow output, whereas others offer wider coverage. Keep in mind that they are bright up close to the subject, but the light falls off as the distance increases, so lights work best when the subject is at a fixed distance.
- **Try to balance artificial lighting with ambient light:** After you establish the distance, adjust the light or camera setting so that the natural and camera light match exposure. Some lights have a dimmer control, which makes it easier to balance them with ambient light. If not, manipulate the balance by adjusting the camera-to-subject distance. The more closely you match the on-camera light with the ambient light of the scene, the more natural it will appear.
- **Be aware of color temperature:** Each source of light differs in output color, varying from the tungsten-balances of 3,200K to 5,600K daylight. That means there can be a difference between a light source on the subject and the rest of the scene. If the camera is set for daylight (5500K) and the light source is tungsten (3200K), the speaker would have an orange color cast, whereas rest of the scene looks normal. The good news is that most include conversion filters to adjust back to tungsten or daylight.

Part IV

Beyond the Webinar

web extras

Visit www.dummies.com for tips on what to do next after the webinar ends.

In this part . . .

- Understand how to build Excel tables that hold and store the data you need to analyze.
- Find quick and easy ways to begin your analysis using simple statistics, sorting, and filtering.
- Get practical stratagems and commonsense tactics for grabbing data from extra sources.
- Discover tools for cleaning and organizing the raw data you want to analyze.

Chapter 13

Continuing the Conversation

In This Chapter

- Reaching out after the presentation
- Realizing that the presentation is just the beginning
- Saying the right thing
- Extending engagement with your audience
- Building a list of interested prospects

The webinar has come to an end, and the presenter has said goodbye to the audience. All things considered, the presentation went pretty well. Now what?

If you're thinking the process is over, you could not be more wrong. In fact, it's just beginning. Consider your favorite recording artist. After all the preparation and work that went into creating their latest album, the process didn't end on the day they released the record. Instead, the band sees it as a new beginning.

Fans can buy the record, and maybe radio stations will play the first single. Websites will host the music video, and the band more than likely will tour in support of the record. The webinar shares a similar evolution. Just because you've wrapped up the presentation doesn't mean that the process comes to a screeching halt. In fact, if it's done right, this is just the beginning.

So how do you continue the conversation? For starters, as soon as the presentation wraps up, you want to push out a survey to find out what the audience thought about the discussion, and whether they had any lingering questions or were looking for specific follow-up information.

Then of course you want to send thank-yous to those who attended and make an attempt to reach out to those who missed it. This gives you another opportunity to provide information on your product or service. In this chapter, I cover ways to continue the conversation after the webinar is over.

Following Up Immediately

It's important to reach out to your attendees after the webinar to build a relationship with them. Not every person who attends your webinar is a seasoned veteran. For many, it's the first time they have ever interacted with your company. They sat through your thought leadership presentation so they have some idea of what you are talking about, but they may not really know what you do. When you want to continue the conversation, it's up to you to follow up with them. By reaching out, you're going to move them further along the sales pipeline, and that's the main goal. Keep in mind, however, there's a fine line between helpful and overly aggressive. So don't come on strong with the sales-speak.

What to do as soon as your webinar ends

After you've hopefully provided the participant with sound and actionable advice and have pushed out the exit survey, you can disconnect from the console. The fun is not over, however. In fact, the next phase of extending the conversation is just beginning.

You can reach out to registrants by doing the following:

- **Send a thank-you e-mail:** Let your webinar attendees know you appreciated their attendance and provide them with your contact information in case they have any follow-up questions or need more information on your product or service. You should send them a link to the on-demand version, too.
- **Reach out to those who missed your presentation:** Send them a different type of thank-you note, one that says something on the order of "Sorry we missed you," as seen in Figure 13-1. Include a link to the on-demand webcast so they can watch it at their leisure and provide your contact information.
- **Invite them to gather more information:** Contact information only goes so far because the attendee may not know what else they want from you. Besides sending the on-demand link, suggest that they download a white paper, schedule a one-on-one conversation with one of your sales experts, or take you up on a free trial offer. Turn the opportunity into an actionable pursuit on their end.

Figure 13-1: Be sure to send the on-demand link to registrants who were not able to attend the webinar.

What information your attendees need

Read any book on etiquette, and you'll see the best way to show people how grateful you are for their wedding gift, a kind gesture, or in this case, webinar attendance. Sending a thank-you to all who registered for and attended you presentation is a great way to get started, but it needs to do more than simply thank them. Instead, use the opportunity to give them more information about your organization and future events.

Consider the following:

- **Contact information:** Make sure you provide the names and contact info of key people in your organization.
- **On-demand link:** I've said it before, and I'll say it again. Be generous with the on-demand link. Send it to everyone, including those who attended so they can either watch it again or pass it on to their colleagues.
- **E-mail address:** It sounds pretty obvious, but don't overlook this important information. Provide a general e-mail address where attendees can send additional questions.
- **Website info:** Be sure the thank-you e-mail includes a link to your website, complete with suggested downloads and other information.

Continue to follow up with attendees

Sending the thank-you note is the first step after your webinar ends, but it's not the only follow-up you need to do. After the webinar, you should go over all the data, looking for signs of unanswered questions or potential sales leads and follow-up with those select participants. Looking at the registration data, poll results, unanswered questions from the Q&A session, and the exit survey provides guidance on how you should reach out to those looking for further assistance.

TIP

Most of the time, you need to initiate contact. Yes, sometimes members of the audience take it upon themselves to ask for more information. Some may take to social media such as Twitter or go into a group on LinkedIn to continue the conversation. But more often than not, after the participant attends the presentation, the conversation stops on their end. That's why it's important for you to monitor social media using the pre-determined hashtag you created for Twitter (as seen in Figure 13-2), Facebook, and the user group on LinkedIn, for starters. You should also check e-mail and surveys.

It's important to follow up with these folks via e-mail and invite them to the next step. If the first step was attending the webinar, the next step may be providing them with additional information, which can include conducting a post-event meeting, or having them attend a product demonstration, if there a product associated with the webinar.

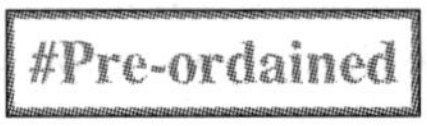

Figure 13-2: Always have a hashtag ready for each presentation.

Extending Engagement

TIP

Registration and webinar data also can extend engagement by ranking your leads. Most companies have a lead-nurturing process that is attached to registrants and attendees. A *lead* is an attendee or registrant who shows some level of interest in your product or services. This nurturing process usually begins as soon as they sign up, and would be automatically filtered into a *marketing automation system*.

Building a list of interested audience members

REMEMBER

Combining participant behavior from the registration process with activity during the webinar helps rank the leads. Otherwise, your presentation will not always include people best suited for your message.

So how does it happen?

It starts with prospective participants signing up for the webinar. The registration form asks attendees for some basic information. This provides key information about the registrant both from their input (such as name, occupation, company, and so on) as well as domain information (knowing the origin of their e-mail address lets you know whether they're associated with a corporation or it's a personal account).

If the registrant attends the presentation, additional data comes from the engagement tools in the console. Here, they answer polls, download stuff, and respond to your exit survey.

Social media provides additional clues. For example, they may post Facebook statuses or tweet during the event. All of that information is recorded, so most webcasting platforms provide detailed analytics for all of these engagement factors. Attendees can easily access a variety of social media tools in the console, as seen in Figure 13-3.

Figure 13-3: Social media choices within the webinar console.

Judging the criteria

If the analytics show that you have one person watching the webcast, that provides a basic lead. But things get more interesting when you have that person watching the webinar and also actively looking for information.

Within the analytics report, you can actually see that this person asked one or more questions via the Q&A button in the console. Maybe they wanted more information on how to do something. Perhaps they want to know where to find the vendor for a particular product you mentioned or to get prices for a service. You should have all of the information on these inquiries.

In your post-webinar analytics report, you can see what they have downloaded. Maybe it was a white paper by a presenter, a copy of the webinar PowerPoint presentation, or perhaps it was a data sheet.

But what does it all mean?

It could mean a lot. For example, if they downloaded a data sheet, it could mean that they are interested in a solution that your product or service can provide for them.

Some providers aggregate this information so you see activity reports and the resources that different people downloaded. However, it's often just a list, so it's up to you how you want to assess that marketing information after the presentation. Still, it's a big help when it comes to building relationships.

All of these factors can be used to qualify different leads:

TIP

- **Questions asked:** You can gauge both individually and collectively the areas that interested your audience the most by examining their questions.
- **Documents downloaded:** What documents were downloaded provides further clues to the topics that interested your attendees most. What they download serves as an indicator of their areas of interest.

TIP

- **Behavior within the console:** How they interacted with the console lets you know what they did while watching the webinar. Did they tweet or post to Facebook? How many questions did they ask? How much (and what) did they download? These stats all provide a snapshot of the participant. More importantly, this information tells you about their behavior during the webinar. The more active they were, the more engaged they likely were with the subject matter.

Offering your webinar on-demand

REMEMBER

Remember how much you love reruns of *Friends* or *Seinfeld*, and the chance to revisit those shows, or maybe see them for the first time? Your registrants may share similar affection for your last webinar, especially if they missed it the first time. Think of on-demand capability as the repeat of your webinar. Not everybody who registered got to see it live. Maybe some of the folks who attended missed a specific point, or wanted to hear it again. It's always a good idea to include an on-demand link from the webinar with all correspondence, regardless of whether the viewer has previously attended.

They might want to watch it again, or some may want to pass it onto colleagues. Offering an on-demand option is a must-have, and don't just put a link in an e-mail either. Post it on your website too. You can offer a selection of on-demand webcasts.

Checking Out the Webinar Academy

Regardless of your level of webinar prowess, it's nice to have a place you turn to when you want to hone your skills. It's even more amazing that you can increase your experience without making the public mistakes that so often accompany learning on the job. And do you know what makes it even sweeter? The certification that comes with finishing each section. That's what one unique online service provides for no cost.

The Webinar Academy (`www.webinaracademy.com`), as seen in Figure 13-4, covers the entire lifecycle of what it takes to create a successful webinar. It offers the opportunity to learn key practices and tactics on four different tracks: producer, promoter, presenter and video. It's a robust virtual environment that hosts a dozen different webinars. There's even a LinkedIn group where you can post questions and have other people respond to them.

The site provides the feel of a virtual space where you can communicate with your peers, ask questions, and view a wealth of resources.

After going through the different tracks and exploring the academy, you can take a test, as seen in Figure 13-5, for certification.

In the next four sections, I cover the four tracks, or sections, of education offered by the Webinar Academy. After completing each 25-minute session, you will have the understanding for putting together your very first, or next, webinar.

Figure 13-4: After you sign up for the Webinar Academy, it brings you the home screen, which resembles a lobby with easy access to different places.

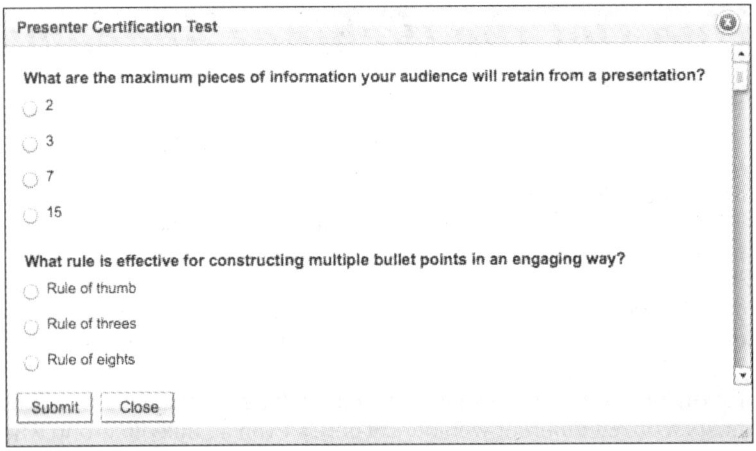

Figure 13-5: A sample test for certification in the Webinar Academy.

Producer Pro track

Whether it's the first, fifth, or twentieth webinar you have produced, there's something here for you. This track thoroughly explains how to plan and execute a webinar from start to finish.

It includes the following sessions:

- Planning Your Webinar
- Integrating with Marketing Automation and CRM
- Creating a Branded Audience Experience
- Effective Lead Scoring

Promoter Pro track

Unless you enroll a thousand participants every time you offer a webinar, there's always something you can learn to bring a few more. This session explains different tactics that can drive registration, increase the attendance ratio of those who register, and effectively promote on-demand viewing.

These sessions include

- Building an On-Demand Strategy
- Social Media Integration
- Creating Compelling Promotions

Presenter Pro track

The finer points of effectively presenting and hosting a webinar are included in these sessions. Learn how to design presentations and interact with an audience during live and on-demand webinars.

These include

- Delivering Interactive Webinars
- Creating Webinar Content
- Using Video in Webinars

Video track

Video can truly bring your webinars to life. The Video Pro track at the Webinar Academy can show you how to make the most of your webinar video.

The twenty-five minute sessions available include

- Introduction to Video Webcasting
- Best Practices for Using Webcams
- Take the Complexity out of Studio Video
- Best Practices for Streaming Video

Chapter 14

Evaluating Your Webinar

In This Chapter

- Critiquing your presentation
- Achieving your goal
- Looking at feedback
- Promoting your on-demand event

The webinar is born on the page, but it comes to life on the stage, so no matter how much you plan and rehearse your special presentation, you can't determine its success until after it's over. Obviously, the more you prepare — and build off of your last webinar — the more you improve your overall presentation.

After the presenter has hit the console button to end the webinar, it's time to evaluate how effectively the presentation was delivered. Think of it as a professional critique of your own show.

A presentation, by and large, is usually a work in progress that improves each time you do it. Evaluating your message when you are doing your first webinar can sometimes warrant drastic changes. But after you have a few webinars under your belt, it's more a matter of adjusting little nuances here and there. Regardless of whether it's your first or fiftieth, you should continually look to see areas where you have room for improvement.

Although going over each presentation with a critical eye can help you perfect it, the biggest indicator remains the audience. You made the webinar for them and see them as your potential customers, so listen to what they're telling you. Combine their feedback with your assessment and what you're learning through the analytics to make sure your message comes through loud and clear.

Analytics play a big part in determining the success of the presentation. So does audience feedback. You can use a variety of methods to make sure that everything in the presentation is moving like a well-oiled machine. In this chapter, I look at some of them.

Reviewing Your Webinar

Although continuing the conversation with your audience is as much of a priority for your organization as windshield wipers on a rainy night are for a driver, it's also important to evaluate the presentation from your own perspective.

With so many parts to the webinar, there's a lot of ground to cover, so it's always a good idea to watch your presentation in its entirety with a critical eye. Remember, there's no substitute for looking at a replay of the event to see how effectively your message was delivered to the audience. Whether you've been producing webinars for a few years, or just cut your teeth on your first one, you'll always find something that you can tweak.

Another part of the assessment process comes from examining the analytics. You should look at all aspects, from registration to the exit survey, to evaluate how well it went.

Being your own harshest webinar critic

Look at the replay of your presentation, as seen in Figure 14-1, as if you were the theater critic for *The New York Times*. You can't be too harsh. Making each of your webinars better than the last, or at least equally as strong, becomes your mission as a producer. Remember, if you don't find the problematic areas, chances are the audience will at some point. If that happens, there's a good chance your attendance will decline.

Figure 14-1: A composite showing the webinar as theater.

When reviewing your webinar, you should pay close attention to the following:

- **Appropriateness of the current format:** Did your chosen format work well with your presentation, or would another have worked more effectively? Would an interview segment have been more effective? Was the moderated panel unruly? All of these questions and answers can help you decide which format works best for your needs.
- **Presenter effectiveness:** The heart and soul of the presentation revolves around the charisma of the speakers. Making sure that the presenter was engaging and each speaker was interesting figures prominently into the equation. If you find a weak link, it's important to change it so that the next presentation is always better.
- **Value of visual assets:** A major part of the webinar centers on your PowerPoint slides, graphics, and images. Keep an eye on how efficiently they're being used. Are the information slides appropriately lean on text? Are the slides on the screen long enough to be read by the audience, but not too long? It's also important to determine how well the graphics and pictures are working for the presentation. Remember, if they don't move the conversation forward, it's probably a good idea to reconsider using them next time around.
- **Effective video use:** Using video tends to increase engagement, but only when it's done correctly. Whether the speaker was properly lit, what video clips were integrated, as seen in Figure 14-2, and whether those clips supported the topic are all important questions for you to ask.
- **Adequate time allowed for each section:** Although scripting and preplanning provide a rough idea of how things will go, it's not until you've actually delivered the webinar that you know whether you've allowed the proper time for each section. Presentations consist of many parts, including the speakers, visual parts, and interactive sections such as the Q&A. Did each have adequate time? Too much time? These are all areas to examine and adjust.
- **Natural flow:** All the planning in the world can't determine how well your webinar flows until after it's completed. So when you view it again on demand, ask yourself if each section segues nicely from one part to the next, or if it's too abrupt or too long. Then make the appropriate changes.

Analyzing the analytics

Review your webcasting reporting analytics like you would look at the baseball box scores the day after the game. Because every part of the webinar process is recorded in some way, these statistics are not hard to find out. Figuring out what to do with them is another story, but that depends on your goal.

Figure 14-2: A music video hosted on the Vimeo website.

For now, start with the following:

- **Registration:** Review the number of people that registered for your current webinar. This will let you know if there's an increase in interest, a decline, or if you're holding steady. With each of these scenarios, you'll know what to do. Here's a hint: If interest is decreasing, work on finding a way to increase it.
- **Attendance:** One indicator of the success of your webinar is an increase in attendance. The more people who are tuning in for your presentation, the more effective your communication and word of mouth obviously are. Don't confuse attendance numbers with registration numbers. Registration is always much higher.
- **On-demand:** When your webinar is done and you've sent the thank-you note and follow-up e-mails with an on-demand link to the webcast, you should also keep an eye on the number of people who watch it on demand. It's something you definitely want to review. It can indicate whether word of mouth is working for you, or whether your participants are repeat-viewing.

Going deeper into analytics

REMEMBER

Although registration and attendance tell you something about the people interested in your topic, the real meat on the bone comes from those who actually attended. The behavior of these folks during the presentation can provide a detailed snapshot of who they are and whether they're prospective customers.

Consider the following:

- **Length of stay:** Of course, you *want* your attendee to stay on until the end of the webcast, but you can't always get what you want. Understanding how long most attendees stay teaches you something about your presentation.
- **Time they logged out:** Some folks are just going to drop off for no apparent reason. That's just the way it is. But when you see a spike at a particular time, as seen on the watch in Figure 14-3, or during a particular section of the presentation, it speaks volumes. You need to investigate whether the drop-off had to do with the speaker, the topic, or time they left. If you see a definite pattern, you should make adjustments for the next presentation.
- **Console activity:** Knowing when the participant decided to call it quits or whether they stayed on for the entire session is important. But equally revealing is how active they were during the time they were logged into the presentation. Analytics gives you a look at their activity (participation in polls, the Q&A, and social media). All of this information provides a better picture for your next webinar, as well as giving you the chance to reach out to particular users.

TIP

Figure 14-3: Time of audience drop-off is a major factor to look at in your webinar.

Listening to the Q&A

If during the Q&A portion of a presentation you asked, "How important is the Q&A to the webinar audience?" the answer would be *overwhelmingly important*. You cannot overstate its value to the audience. It's equally significant to the producer, but for a different reason.

The questions asked — whether there was time to answer them during the presentation or not — can let you know exactly what the participants are interested in, and not just within the context of the webinar. The questions asked can also tell you what people want to know about your product or service.

Sometimes their questions can indicate their interest in your company. Or maybe they ask about something that you didn't realize was important and can use as the topic in your next presentation. Either way, reviewing the questions helps you evaluate your webinar.

Staying on Goal

Although every webinar has a goal, not every goal can be met in 58 minutes. That forces you to make sure that all the key information you want to tell the audience — and all that they desire — is presented within your timeframe. Unfortunately, it doesn't always work that way.

In the scripting and rehearsal phase, you can make sure that the meatiest parts of the topic are properly discussed and that your core message is apparent, but what you cannot anticipate is the audience interaction part. Sometimes their interests are slightly different than what you're presenting. You can discover this from the polls and the Q&A, mostly, but also on social media.

It's essential to stick to your goal. That mainly has to do with the presentation and the speaker. You want to make sure that everything within that presentation covers your intended topic as much as possible. If not, you can continue the conversation by sending follow-up e-mails — even after you send the thank-you e-mails. Put any missing or incomplete topics in there to make sure your audience gets what you promised.

Is the presenter properly steering the discussion?

A certain failure-to-launch occasionally plagues some speakers. Maybe they're navigating rough waters, like those seen in Figure 14-4, and they're simply having a bad day, or a particular audience is just not feeling it. The reason doesn't matter, but it's up to you to always make sure that your speaker has delivered all that was promised in your promotional materials. If you notice that the speaker missed some key information, or analytics determine that the audience wanted to hear more on a certain topic, you need to do something about it. If something is missing, you can follow up with attendees via e-mail, for example.

Figure 14-4: A pilot boat navigating rough waters.

Did the slides work?

REMEMBER

Although the presentation is always about the speaker, it's the slides that help support main topics of the conversation by showing a visual reminder to the audience. It's possible to show too many slides or sometimes too few, however. These are more obvious issues, but subtler issues with your slides can plague you too.

If any of the following happened during your last presentation, make sure it doesn't happen during the next one:

- A slide wasn't on-screen long enough for anyone besides a speed-reader to read it.
- You used too many bullet points. If they're on a majority of your text slides, or if you have more than five bullets on a single one, well, then that's too many.
- The slide contradicted or was unrelated to what the speaker was saying.

It's All about Performance

At the end of the day, the success of the webinar depends on the strength of the performance. Not just from the presenters — although they play a big part — but also regarding the content within each topic.

The presenter has the starring role in the webinar, and it's up to her to deliver the topic in an entertaining way that keeps the audience engaged.

It's important that the speaker can engage the audience not only with her presence, but also on a functional level. For example, she needs to push out polls like the one shown in Figure 14-5 during the webcast, answer the Q&A questions, and participate in group chat.

If the presenter and other speakers can engage the attendees, you're going to maintain their attention for most of the session, if not all of it. That's always one of your main goals.

To make sure the audience stays engaged in the discussion, ask the following questions:

- **Presenter:** Was the presenter engaging from start to finish? If not, where was the lull? Was the presenter properly attired?
- **Speaker:** Did each speaker accurately answer the audience's questions? Or did they answer in such a way that raised new questions?
- **Polls:** How quickly did the presenter push out the polls? Were they relevant? Was the audience response satisfactory?
- **Q&A:** Was there enough time to answer questions during the presentation?
- **PowerPoint:** How effective were the slides in relation to the topic?

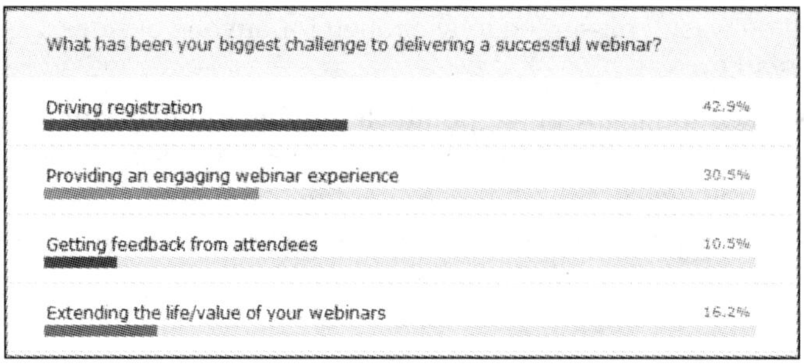

Figure 14-5: The results of a poll taken during a webinar.

Getting Immediate Feedback

All of the analytics and e-mails in the world can't offer the immediate feedback that you get during the Q&A session. Q&A provides the most immediate measure of the discussion because the questions are being asked live.

Not only does it keep the topic you're discussing relevant, but it also lets you know what's possibly missing. For example, if the webinar covers X and Y and the people have questions about Z, it gives the presenter an opportunity to address that topic, time permitting.

However, if presenters cannot answer those questions within the timeframe of the presentation, they provide the speaker or company presenting the webinar with another opportunity to expand on their topics. Maybe something touched on in discussion needs to be explained further. That helps guide the conversation down the road, maybe for another webcast focusing on the second topic.

Gauging audience experience

Sometimes the most overlooked aspect of evaluating your webinar is the audience experience. Did they get everything they wanted from the discussion? Was there enough time to ask questions? Did they find the console user-friendly enough to operate? But most importantly, you need to make sure that the overall user experience was positive. You can derive all of this information through the analytical tools from the provider. That's why it's so important to have a user-friendly console. This way, the participant is motivated to use it.

Fixing any problems ASAP

When the participant experiences problems, they must be resolved immediately. For example, if someone uses the chat box to let the presentation team know that they cannot hear the presenter or some part of the presentation, they should receive a response within 30 seconds providing them with some assistance. The answer may be as simple as telling them to refresh their browser to see if that fixes the problem.

If the simple suggestions are not working, somebody needs to address the problem immediately — just not the speaker. Maybe you need a producer-type person on the back end helping to solve any problems that the audience is experiencing. Never leave the audience hanging. If they drop off, chances are that they won't be coming back.

Using chat in the webinar

Group communication remains as crucial to the webinar experience as bread is to a PB&J. Chat creates a virtual environment that allows the audience to network and interact with one another, virtually.

Chat creates a great dialogue between the audience and the presenter as well as among the audience members, as seen in Figure 14-6. But sometimes it can create an unruly situation, or at least one that detracts from the presentation. That's when the audience chats amongst themselves and stops paying attention to the presenter.

That can definitely be a factor when you have thousands of people on a webcast and you open a group chat. It's not something you can really monitor effectively, especially if ten people are typing comments at the same time. Group chat is something to be used in certain circumstances, mostly smaller webinars. It's probably not a good idea for the bigger ones because group chat can be disruptive.

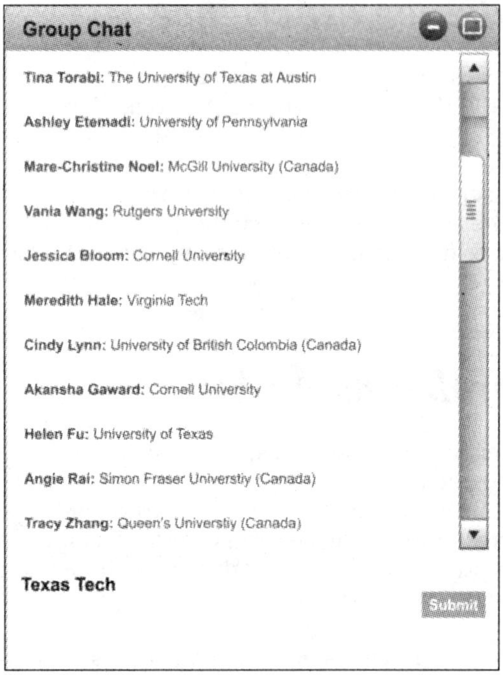

Figure 14-6: Group chat activity.

Examining Analytics

Webinar software provides detailed analytics that lets you evaluate audience behavior to determine your webinar's success. It's important to look at the data to find ways to better serve your audience. Through their habits during the presentation, the audience gives you many indicators of both the success of your presentation and what they want moving forward. Sometimes it's about the next webinar, but more importantly, it's about being a nice match for your product and services.

Here are some areas to look at:

- **Attendance conversion rate:** This stat looks at the number of attendees as opposed to registrants. Was it higher than the average 42 percent conversion rate ratio of those that register and attend? Or was it lower?
- **Participant duration:** How long did participants stay on, and when did they drop off? Evaluate when they dropped off. If they dropped off ten minutes into the presentation, maybe there is something you can tweak in the beginning to make it more engaging. You have to evaluate why people dropped off.
- **On-demand viewers:** Look at how many people viewed your webinar on-demand. You can also see whether people viewed it on-demand the first time, or whether they actually viewed it live and watched again on-demand. If someone views it on-demand *and* live, they're demonstrating obvious interest in your product or message.

Continue to Promote Your On-Demand Event

Remember, the life of your webinar goes beyond its live performance. As long as you're offering an on-demand version, you should continue to promote it. It is a common mistake for companies hosting on-demand webcasts to stop all promotions after the live event is over. But that content, along with your other archived webinars, still has a lot of value and should still be promoted to audiences that could benefit from viewing it.

That doesn't mean you should keep promoting the same event over and over again. Instead, try a staggered approach (featuring a different archived event) each week. That provides the best opportunity to catch prospective viewers at a period of interest or receptivity.

More About On-Demand

Today's audiences value convenience and control. They want to consume content their way — anytime, anywhere, and on any device. On-demand webinars meet these needs perfectly. An apt comparison is the DVR. People increasingly record their favorite TV shows to watch at their convenience or even multiple times. If you're a *Game of Thrones* fan, you know what I mean!

Chapter 15

Preparing for Your Next Webinar

In This Chapter

- Optimizing your presentation
- Tweaking each performance
- Increasing the scope of your webinar
- Creating a webinar series

Say you've got your first webinar under your belt, or your tenth — it really doesn't matter. It's time to prepare for your next one. Maybe you already have a topic planned, a script started, and a few speakers lined up, and hey, that's great. But in order to make the next one better, you need to analyze the last one to see what — if anything — you can improve.

Chances are that you can tweak a few things. Maybe you can make modifications to the overall format or to individual sections. But more importantly, looking at the presentation with a critical eye helps keep you in tune.

You also want to look at how effectively your host and speakers are engaging the audience, especially if it's an ongoing thing. Running a webinar series shares much in common with being a television executive in that you constantly look at how well the show is received by its viewers. But instead of relying on the more passive Nielsen ratings that networks rely on, you have the benefit of real-time analytics and feedback.

Resetting Your Goals

The main objective of any presentation relies on keeping your audience engaged while at the same time delivering your message. With the webinar, it's engagement that trumps everything. Don't be shocked. No matter how informative your message is, if you can't get the audience to stay tuned for its duration, it doesn't matter what you had to say. They can't hear your message if they're not tuning in.

Make no mistake; engagement is the first order of business. So when you're evaluating your webinar and the analytics that go along with it, it's important to find out which factors kept the audience engaged and which may have caused a drop-off in interest. Quite simply, it's a matter of accentuating the positive and eliminating the negatives.

Promoting and tracking your leads

Adopt a dog, and chances are she has a tracking chip implanted that helps you find her if she gets lost. Wouldn't it be cool if we could put a chip in our correspondence with leads? Oh, wait a minute — that's already possible.

When promoting your next presentation, you can embed a tracking code in the invitation, as well as other places, so you can track exactly where your audience base has originated. These codes go by several different names, such as *partner reference ID* or a *campaign tracking ID*, and typically are embedded in all the links that you are distributing across the various platforms to which you're trying to drive registration. Each possible source gets a unique registration link.

Most marketing automation services provide analytical tracking information. You can also do it yourself by creating an account using Google Analytics (`www.google.com/analytics`).

Although these codes cannot find your lost participants for you, they can track the origin of your registrants and attendees, providing answers about where your registrant came from. Here are some of the possibilities:

- E-mail
- Banners you had on your website
- Social media efforts
- Paid search efforts
- Individual e-mails from sales reps to customers and prospects
- A referral link from others who signed up and then referred other people to you

Accentuating the positive

It's important to look at exactly what drove people to your webinar. After you determine where most of your leads come from, or where they are not coming from, you can prioritize the different channels that resulted in higher numbers of registrants.

You may discover that you got great results from an e-mail blast that promoted a specific angle. For example, maybe the webinar invitation that featured a certain guest speaker was the one that more people responded to, rather than the one that was a more generic view of the topic.

Conversely, you obviously would want to optimize or minimize the types of outreach that are not working well.

Making an Improvement Plan

I wouldn't be so drastic as to say that if you're not moving ahead, you're falling behind, but the objective is certainly to get better each time. No one campaigns for *lower* awareness or to *worsen* morale. The objective is always to move forward, and when it comes to your last webinar, you need to analyze it to see how it compares with your current goals. When there is a disparity, you want to make adjustments.

Do you know what would be odd? If a company said they wanted fewer people to attend their next presentation, or wanted lower sales for the next quarter. Don't expect anyone producing a webinar to want to hold steady or decrease attendance. After all, getting as many people to see your presentation is the main objective. The more folks who attend your presentation, the more potential partners, customers, and prospects will come your way.

So how do you increase attendance? Well, there are a few ways.

Finding out where attendees came from

You can see the people who registered for the event as well as the specific efforts that led them to you from your campaign tracking analytics. In addition, you can also see whether any of those efforts translated into an unusually high registrant-to-attendee rate. For example, was it your e-mail marketing campaign that drove them to register in droves, or did most of your traffic come from a web banner? The same applies to areas that were not as productive.

Here are a few areas to look at when it comes to finding what brings an audience to you:

TIP

- **E-mail:** Determine the effectiveness of your e-mail campaign and how many registrants it brought to you. Because e-mail is a major avenue for promotion, you may want to delve further into the analytics to see where there were differences in results.
- **Repeat attendees:** Are you getting repeat offenders at your webinars? (And by offenders, I mean attenders . . . er, attendees.) If so, it tells you that you're doing something right.
- **Cross-mentions in another webinar:** Sometimes you can include a shout-out to your next webinar in your current presentation. Or maybe you have a regularly scheduled series and provide "coming attraction" announcements about what you plan next. If it has helped, it's nice to know.
- **Word of mouth:** On your registration form, it's common to ask the registrants how they found out about the webinar. Although you may not know where the referral came from, it's a positive sign whenever your previous attendees are spreading your message through word of mouth, as seen in Figure 15-1.

TIP

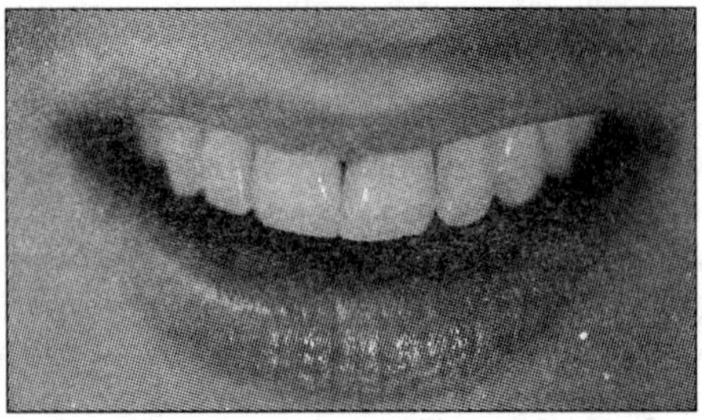

Figure 15-1: Word of mouth is one of the best ways to promote your webinar.

Aggressively improving the registrant-attendee ratio

REMEMBER

Approximately 42 percent of people who register for your webinar actually show up for the presentation, according to the ON24 Webinar Benchmarks report. That's like inviting 10 people to a party and having only 4.2 of them show up. (To say nothing of how disturbing it would be if two-tenths of a person showed up at a party.)

It's nice to have more people in attendance. After all, that's why you invited them in the first place. An internal webcast for employees of a large corporation naturally will have a much higher turnout mainly because attendance is usually mandatory. Fee-based webinars also have a high attendance rate for obvious reasons. People tend to take commitments more seriously when they've paid for them.

But when you're reaching out to the public, you're going to have far more registrants than attendees. Some have the best intentions of making it, and then something comes up. Other times, it simply slips their mind. So although achieving a 100 percent attendance rate at your next webinar is about as likely as you winning the lottery, you still want to increase the attendance rate as much as you can.

E-mail remains the main mechanism for getting the word out on your upcoming webinar, and also for reminding registrants. Try experimenting with modifying your reminders.

TIP

It is common practice to send a reminder one week before the event, and another on the day it takes place. Interestingly enough, that last e-mail reminder can raise attendance by 20 percent or more. This begs the question: If you send more reminders, will that optimize attendance?

It's the kind of thing you have to experiment with based on your particular audience. There's a fine line between reminding registrants of your upcoming event and annoying them with countless e-mails. You want to experiment with exactly how many reminder e-mails you can send without being disruptive.

REMEMBER

Consider whether you are getting results from your e-mail blasts. If they are not working, ease up on the reminders. Otherwise, they typically produce a curve that has a diminishing return.

Observing audience behavior

REMEMBER

Almost everything in life has a cause and effect. If you leave a saucer of milk outside your back door for the local stray cat, guess what will happen? That local stray cat will keep coming back for more.

The same can apply to your audience. You just have to figure out what they want from your presentation. Finding what they want often comes from observing their behavior, much like the graphic seen in Figure 15-2.

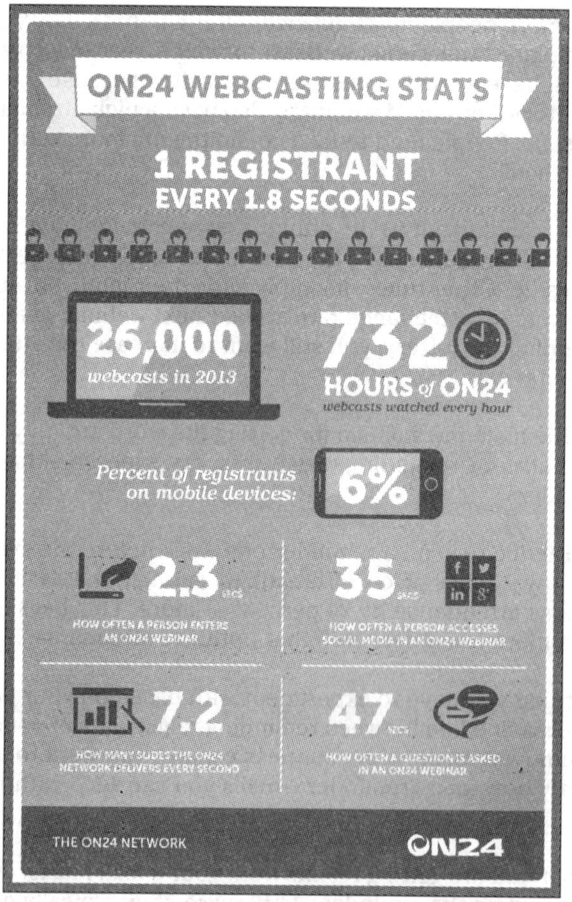

Figure 15-2: A webcasting statistics graphic.

TIP

Behaviors to keep an eye on include

- **Increased activity:** Maybe a certain speaker or segment shows increased activity on chat or social media.
- **Lure of the speaker:** Many participants come to your webinar because of a particular speaker. Sometimes it's obvious — like if your speaker is a big name — but other times, it has more to do with the participants activity during a speaker's performance that lets you know. For example, it's a positive sign when attendees tweet a speaker's comments during the webinar.

- **What your audience is asking:** The Q&A says so much about what the audience wants, not just a particular question, but even beyond the entire presentation. For example, pay attention to when they ask about products and services, or when they ask questions that go beyond the topic.
- **Exit survey:** By using exit surveys, you can assess what your audience thought about the presentation and what else they expect.

It's equally important to find out how long they stayed logged on to the webinar. Was it for the entire duration, or did they give up at a certain point?

Some of the common reasons attendees leave early include

TIP

- **Certain time spans:** Look for a spike in drop-offs after specific times. Maybe it's half past the hour, or when crossing into the next half hour. Sometimes it has to do with engagement over a longer period as people lose interest. Other times, it's more random.
- **Lull in activity:** Too many talky passages or boring speakers can act as viewer-repellant. Look for patterns when they're leaving. For example, did you lose a lot of people when a certain speaker came on? Were there too many slides, or not enough? Although you won't always know for sure, if the analytics show a drop-off happens during a specific period, it's safe to say you need to reassess next time around.

TIP

- **Lengthy timeframe:** It's important to assess if people are dropping off due to the length of your webinar. Maybe there's a big drop-off when you cross from a half hour to 40 minutes. Or did breaking the one-hour mark cause them to say "no mas?" According to ON24's 2013 Benchmark Survey, the average time attending a webinar is 54 minutes.

Developing a Bigger Plan

REMEMBER

After you complete your first webinar — and you take the process and analysis seriously — you're most likely going to want to make the next one bigger and better. The same holds true if you've done a few. You can offer more specific subject matter, or perhaps even start a series.

Building from your first webinar

TIP

Whew! You got that first one under your belt, and probably learned a few things you didn't know until now. Are you taking advantage of the trends, as shown in Figure 15-3? At this point, you still have some tweaking to do to get it just right.

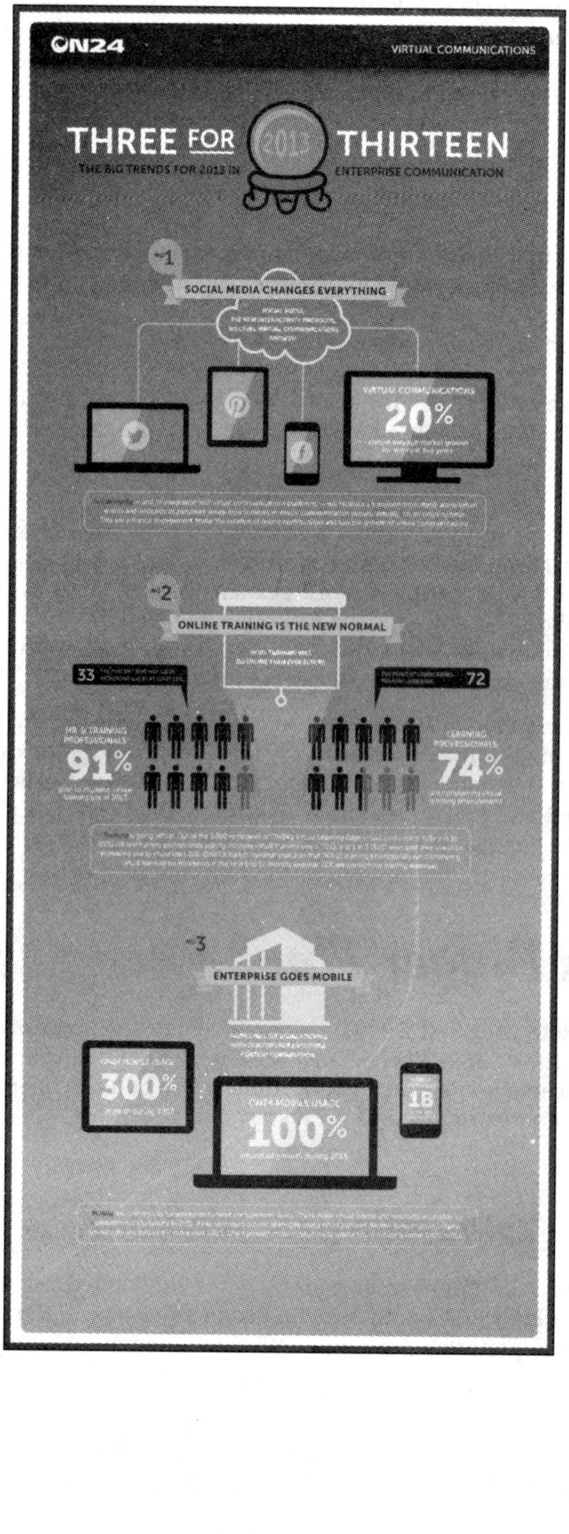

Figure 15-3: Trends in enterprise communication.

You should look at the following aspects and see where you can improve your webinar:

- **Promotion:** Are you promoting from two to three different angles, such as the profile of the speaker, the value proposition of the speaker, or value proposition of the topic?
- **Format:** Make sure the format works with your topic. If all you need is a single speaker, make sure he is engaging. If you're a beginner, be careful to avoid complex formats that you're not ready to handle yet.
- **Ample Q&A:** Did everyone get a chance to ask questions? If not, extend the period. Statistics show that Q&A is one of the reasons that participants stay tuned in.
- **Timeframe:** Do you have enough content for the timeframe? If not, shorten your presentation so there's no filler.
- **Good follow-up:** Make sure you send a thank-you and an on-demand link to everyone who registered.

Creating a series

If you created a television series, you would make sure there was a consistency throughout each show, from the lead actors to the theme song. It's the same when you want to produce a regularly scheduled webinar.

To establish consistency, consider the following:

- **Frequency and time slot:** It's effective to build a rhythm into your webinar by having a specific time slot. Make it like appointment TV — you know, TV you make an appointment to watch because you can't miss it — and hold it on a certain day and time, like maybe every other Thursday at 10 a.m. The idea is to create a time slot your audience — over time — will get accustomed to so that you can bring their attention to whatever it is that you want to tell them.
- **Program length:** Try to maintain a consistent length, so people know how much time they need to attend your webinar. If you plan on having 30 minutes of content, make the duration 45 minutes to have enough time for Q&A and housekeeping.
- **Consistent graphics:** The visual part of the presentation should use consistent graphics on the PowerPoint slides, your promotional material, the landing page, and on the webinar console. Make sure that you brand it so people understand that this is a series hosted by the same company. That's the way to start shaping preferences: by people reacting to your brand.

- **Use the same host:** It's also a good idea to have a consistent host, just so there is one consistent voice that carries across. That voice can bring in different subjects.

Considering format changes

Companies are all over the place when it comes to format, so think of it from the audience perspective. Some people are engaging with webinars because of the content, and they know out of the gate that this is going to be ongoing. If that is the case, you should probably create a predictable format and stick with it so people know exactly what they are going to get when they tune into the webinar.

Many companies use webinars for marketing purposes. In that case, you're adjusting the format to the message that you want to push out that particular time. Sometimes the topic will lend itself to a product demo. Sometimes it lends itself to having an analyst on the call, if it's a thought-leadership message you want to showcase. Other times, you may want to bring in your CEO or leadership team for some type of announcement. You will typically adjust the format to the content you're presenting. When it comes to marketing webinars, the content and the scope of what you want to communicate will typically vary, and thus the format will change accordingly.

You want to maintain a predictable format because you want to begin shaping preferences. You need to stay consistent in order to do that. That doesn't mean you cannot modify it when it's really necessary. How much you can actually change it depends on the temperament of the audience. For example, if you change the discussion from a panel to an interview format, that seems reasonable, but it's not as reasonable to abruptly change from a weekly panel to a single speaker. But overall, you want to shape a webinar into something people will tune into, so you need to build in a certain level of predictability.

If you're doing a regularly scheduled webinar, say once a month, you may not want to make any dramatic changes from time to time, unless you're getting a really clear signal that change is required. Instead, look at trend lines little by little and then make changes as needed to optimize your webcast results.

Part V
The Part of Tens

Visit www.dummies.com for ten (more or less) tips on shooting effective video.

In this part . . .

- Understand how to build Excel tables that hold and store the data you need to analyze.
- Find quick and easy ways to begin your analysis using simple statistics, sorting, and filtering.
- Get practical stratagems and commonsense tactics for grabbing data from extra sources.
- Discover tools for cleaning and organizing the raw data you want to analyze.

Chapter 16

Ten Tips for Successful Webinars

In This Chapter

- Understanding the value of adequate preparation
- Knowing the importance of rehearsal
- Getting cozy with your audience

With so many pieces to make work together for every webinar, things are bound to go wrong sometimes. So, until you can eliminate the possibility of an embarrassing image popping up while you're speaking or the program not going as planned, it's important to go over your upcoming webinar with a fine-toothed comb.

All the audience needs is a computer screen or mobile device to see you. The only problem is that you can't see them. You see, there's a void created when you don't see your audience.

When you're up in front of an audience, you can see their faces, their body language. That allows you to temper the conversation to hold interest. But with a webinar, you're often unaware of the number of folks it's reaching and you don't get that immediate visual feedback on your audience's reaction. As a result, you're speaking into the abyss. And although night-vision goggles won't help you see any better, here are some helpful hints that will let you move through the darkness like a bat in a belfry.

Drive Registration to the Top

The most basic rule for success in the brick-and-mortar world is "location, location, location," but when it comes to maximizing webinar registration, it's all about timing.

Some times are more convenient than others, so by choosing prime times, or avoiding "bad" ones, you can assure your webcast has the most attendees.

So what do you need to know? Avoid Mondays and Fridays — these are peak meeting days and attendance is therefore often lower. According to a leading industry analyst, the best time of the day is 1 p.m. EST because it also accommodates attendees on the west coast. Many webcasts and virtual events are hosted between 11 a.m. EST and 3 p.m. EST.

Here are some others ways to increase registration:

- **Fully utilize your own database:** Don't just depend on external lists aimed at specific attendees when it comes to publicizing virtual events. You should also tap into your internal database and tell your friends, colleagues, and other clients. Experts agree that about 70 percent of all virtual event registrations are the result of promoting to internal lists.
- **Give yourself plenty of time:** It takes a lot to plan and carry out a successful webcast, so start the process at least four weeks before a webcast and 12 weeks before a virtual show.
- **Focus on key areas:** Development of a compelling topic, identification of presenters and the target audience, and a promotional outreach campaign all take time to properly flush out. They're also key to the success of the event.
- **Maximize impact and ROI:** Match your messages to your audience. Understand the interests of your registrants; doing so provides great insight into the audience's priorities.

Plan, Plan, Plan . . . and Then Plan Some More

REMEMBER

Although there's no shortage of theories when it comes to the secrets of success, one thing is certain: Poor planning will always lead to poor production. Even mediocre planning can lead to poor production, and things don't get much better with haphazard, moderate, or occasional planning. Be sure to plan your words and assets each time.

Breaking it down, you need to concentrate on each of these areas, both separately and together:

- **Schedule:** Make sure you have a tightly scheduled program with the appropriate amount of time allotted for each segment. You also need to take into consideration the type of format you're using for the webinar.
- **Have a Great Script and Stick to It:** It's nearly impossible to cover each topic in a limited time by ad-libbing. That's why it's imperative to proceed with a tightly written script. When you find the words and images that strike the right tone, lock them down. That's not to say

you shouldn't correct small errors or change words for clarity. But you should consider your script done at some point so that you can move on to the next step: executing it successfully.

- **PowerPoint presentation:** Make sure it works and all the slides are in proper order.
- **Q&A period:** Figure out how much time you're going to need to sufficiently answer questions. Keep in mind that allowing too little time will not satisfy your audience, but also be aware that allowing too much time leads to a lull.
- **Video:** Consider how you plan to use video. Besides showing the speaker, you can also show clips to support your topics, either from your hard drive, or a video site like YouTube or Vimeo. Also consider whether you want the presenter to use a webcam or more sophisticated video equipment and so on. All of these things factor in.

Rehearse with Your Slides, Graphics, and Video

TIP

Since the beginning of time — or perhaps some time after the invention of the Gutenberg printing press — pictures have done a good job of supporting words. But there's nothing more embarrassing during a webinar than a malfunction with your slides or video.

Don't just check: Double-check. And if double-checking is your style, triple-check it too. Remember, the time you spend now may save you a great deal of embarrassment later.

Consider the following:

- **Use a remote:** If you let the show run automatically, the wrong slide can pop up. Even if it belongs in the presentation, it may come up before or after you expected it. Use a remote to manually change slides.
- **Take it slow in rehearsal:** The first time you rehearse, just be concerned about getting everything right. Don't worry about timing; just make sure your words match up well with the slides. If they don't, make new ones that work.

TIP

- **Display an introductory slide:** Provide viewers with webinar information, including the start time. Let it stay up until the designated start time.
- **Be sure your content is accurate:** If you're showing screen grabs of website addresses or other addresses or factual information, check it all before you go live with the slide.

Be Entertaining and Make Sure Your Host and Speakers Are, Too

Think back to your public school principal's long-winded speeches. Lectures without an entertaining component aren't fun. Don't make your webinar experience boring for your audience. Instead, think of some appropriate funny stories and anecdotes, and be sure not to talk for long stretches without breaking it up with other content.

- **Have a script but be spontaneous too:** When you have a clear idea of the direction of the session, you can make a spontaneous remark now and then without veering off-track.
- **Less is more:** Part of being entertaining is knowing when not to drone on.
- **Keep it moving:** Don't get stuck on a single topic. Give it the proper time and then move along. If you feel that a topic necessitates further discussion but you've already used its allotted time, tell the audience they can revisit it by asking about it during the Q&A period.
- **Use humor:** Always be prepared for spontaneous opportunities to liven things up with humor, but it doesn't hurt to write a few jokes into the show. Just make sure they're clever, relevant, and not offensive. Remember, you're reaching across the Internet. Something harmless in your neck of the woods can be offensive somewhere else.

Know Your Audience and Appeal to Them

If you're older than 25 and recently attended a One Direction concert, you may have realized two things. One, that the band understands how to appeal to their audience, generally made up of young, screaming teenage girls. Two, *you* are most likely not the intended audience. So although your little sister, daughter, or other loved one enjoyed the show, you're simply happy that they're happy. The moral of the story is that every performer has his audience, and success lies in understanding what they want.

Here are some aspects to consider:

- **Make content your number-one priority:** Offer content that matches your audience's needs, demographics, and interests. Make sure your meeting content is truly compelling. Interesting, informative content is the single most critical element required for your virtual meeting's success.

- **Don't assume they're like you:** Huh? This applies to so many things, from realizing that your audience probably doesn't understand the subject as well as you do to accepting that they may not share your sense of humor, to a dozen other things. Your views on politics, morals, religion, and other such sentiments should be kept to yourself.
- **Research the culture:** If you know a majority of your audience is from the southwestern part of the country, for example, be sure to tailor the show to them and prepare analogies that make them feel comfortable. Don't use a lot of analogies about traffic in midtown Manhattan when your audience has never experienced that and can't relate.
- **Choose topics that you know:** There's a beautiful synergy when you combine your area of expertise with what your audience wants to hear.
- **Be aware of gestures:** They're often not as universal as you think. Depending on where you are, they mean different things. For example, giving the OK sign at a seminar in the United States communicates in the affirmative with your fellow Americans. Make that same sign in front of a Brazilian audience, and they will not see it the same way. In their culture, it has the same impact as sticking up your middle finger to a group of Americans.

Interact with Your Audience Before, During, and After

All too often we forget the *social* in social media. Be sure to engage your audience throughout the process. That means more than just during the presentation, but during the time leading up to it, as well as the follow-up period.

Remember the following:

- **Let your audience know what you're doing:** Send out e-mail announcements a month or so before your webinar.
- **Use social media:** Use Twitter and Facebook to remind your audience about the webinar. Then tease them with a preview of what they can expect.
- **Summarize during the webinar:** Recap what's happened so far. You could do a summary at the halfway point, or highlight an aspect of the webinar.
- **Get feedback:** At the end of your webinar, check in with your participants to find out what they thought.

Use Presentation Slides and Images to Support the Theme

TIP

If a picture is truly worth a thousand words, using some well-placed images and information can increase the message to the second power, and do so without boring the audience. Remember, the multimedia aspect is what separates a webinar from a conference call. Take advantage of using as much illustrative material as it takes to make your point effectively.

Rehearse Your Webinar as if It Were a Broadway Play

REMEMBER

Somewhere between preparing your lines for a community theater production of Arthur Miller's *All My Sons*, and getting the words and delivery just right for Stephen Sondheim's "Getting Married Today" lies the intensity of rehearsing for your webinar.

TIP

Just like both of those theater gems, the objective is to make every word and action like second nature. That can only come with practice and rehearsal.

To get it just right, try the following:

- Get comfortable with each section.
- Don't worry about timing until you get comfortable with the content.
- Do a complete dry run at whatever pace you're comfortable, and then gradually pick up the pace.

Understand the Material as if Your Life Depended on It

REMEMBER

Okay, maybe thinking that your life depends on this is a touch extreme, but only if you don't want to sound convincing. Regardless of whether you're running the webinar, presenting it, or playing a small role, it's in your best interest to do your homework.

Tips for doing this include

- **Be sure to understand the topic:** Sometimes we all think we know a topic, only to find that we can't answer questions from a different perspective. For example, what if you were doing a talk on fantasy football and told the audience in a points-per-reception league that it's important to draft a particular type of wide receiver, and then in the Q&A portion someone asks you to explain the difference between a slot and possession receiver, and you couldn't? Not good.

TIP

- **Practice pronunciations:** It's never reassuring when you're perceived as an authority and then you mispronounce important words and phrases. Take the time and practice saying them in advance.
- **Economize your words:** In other words, get to the point.
- **Understand your content:** Be sure that you understand the connection between your words and pictures on-screen. Double-check them, and if there's a shred of doubt, go for the trifecta and do it again.

Gather Feedback and Make Your Next Webinar Better

REMEMBER

Communication, in general, is an evolving process. Answers to questions ranging from "Is my hair getting thinner?" to "Do these jeans make me look fat?" help us grow. (Actually, be careful with the latter one — the wrong answer could temporarily end communication. But I digress.)

When it comes to building a better webinar, much of the process is rooted in making improvements to the last one. The only way you can successfully do that is to reach out to your audience.

Because word of mouth is less effective thanks to the very nature of a webinar, it's important to learn the good, the bad, and ugly about the webinar you just broadcast so that you can continuously shape your message.

Consider these:

- **Online polls:** Get the attendees' feedback during and after the webcast by conducting a poll.
- **Exit survey:** Exit surveys provide the opportunity for a quick assessment of the webinar. It also allows your audience to rank the overall webinar, as well as rate the topics.

TIP

- **Expanded communication:** Polls and surveys are great, but their multiple-choice nature can let some information slip through the cracks. Having a message board or dedicated e-mail address provides a forum for communication with those who have more to say.

Chapter 17

Ten Common Webinar Mistakes and How to Avoid Them

In This Chapter

- Failing to promote your webinar in advance
- Disrespecting your audience's time
- Failing to prepare for on demand

If 99 things go right in your webinar, and only one thing goes wrong, that one wrong thing is what people will remember. No surprise there, because it's the same in everyday life, whether it's at home or on the job. Your webinar is not exempt. In fact, there's some added drama because the meeting is held online without the presenter directly facing the audience. Give them a reason to lose confidence, and they're out of there quicker than a raccoon in your trash bin as you walk up the driveway.

That's a little different than what happens at a physical meeting. It's less likely for someone to walk out of a physical meeting because of a minor glitch. Their peers' eyes are upon them. But when it comes to webinar problems, you can bet that your participants will web-surf, walk away from the screen, or worse, log out.

But not all problems are related to the actual presentation. In fact, many mistakes are made in the early stages and resonate until the end. In order to put on a successful webinar and draw the most participants, it's important to understand the common mistakes and avoid them upfront.

Thinking a Single Promotion Is a Good Idea

If your dental hygienist didn't send a reminder for your next cleaning as the date drew near, chances are you could forget the appointment. The same holds true for a webinar. Unfortunately, some marketers send out their e-mail list just once and settle for the results. Studies show that attendance can increase when sending multiple e-mails at least seven days before the event.

Although it's commonplace for some organizations to kick off a webinar in seven days or less, it's usually not a good idea. This approach involves sending the invitation a week before the webinar and then following up a few days before. But studies show that audience size increases by 36 percent when you start promoting the event more than one week before.

TIP

By changing to a two-week promotional strategy, you can bring in more participants as well as work several angles to register them. Your first invitation could be HTML — that's when it's formatted like a web page and includes pictures, graphics, and color — and focus on the event at a high level. The second might be plain text — less razzle-dazzle, but certainly readable on any device — that zeroes in on featured speakers or content. The art of driving webinar registration is all about catching people at a moment of receptivity with a message that resonates with them. Extending webinar promotions beyond a week and delivering multiple messages and e-mail types increase your chance of successfully hitting that moment of receptivity.

Failing to Have an Optimized Registration and Confirmation Page

Here's an alarming statistic: Fewer than half of the people who begin registering for your webinar will complete the registration form. That means marketers are losing more than half their prospective audience members at the point of registration. And what's driving them away? It's the registration page itself. This failure to optimize registration (and confirmation) pages is easy to fix after you recognize the problem.

Here are some ways to get your potential attendees to follow through on registration:

WARNING!

- **Avoid lengthy registration forms:** Nobody likes filling out lengthy forms, yet some organizations think that it's a good idea to ask for far more information than they really need. Busy customers take one look at these long forms, decide they will be too time-consuming, and exit the registration process. Don't make the mistake of scaring off your audience with overly complicated registration forms. Just ask for basic demographic information such as company, name, title, industry, revenue, and contact information. This is enough information to determine if the prospect is right for you, but not so much information that prospective attendees will get turned off and quit.

- **Embedding helpful tools:** They enable registrants to place your webinar on their existing business calendar increases the likelihood of them attending the live event.
- **Inconsistent creative expectation:** The old "bait and switch" has become so commonplace that prospective participants need reassurance. Attendees need visual confirmation that the event for which they are registering is the same event they saw in the promo, but often there is a visual mismatch from promotion to registration. Avoid this potential miscommunication by assuring your prospects they are in the right place. Use consistent creative information on every page, including consistent pictures, icons, and logos. Make sure those items are on e-mails, registration pages, and landing pages.
- **Don't forget about the confirmation page:** That's the page that tells them they've successfully registered. Many promoters don't take advantage of it, but there's so much you can do with one. Think about it: When you buy something online, e-commerce retailers confirm your purchase, and then offer you other opportunities such as purchasing a similar product. But not all webinar producers have caught up with this concept, thereby limiting the growth of their audience and brand. The confirmation page is the perfect place to grow your audience numbers by telling them about your upcoming events.

Try the following to help maximize your present and future webinar attendance:

- **Tell your audience about upcoming events:** Provide blurbs and links to upcoming webinars.
- **Have them subscribe to you:** If you have a newsletter or other online information, share that with them.
- **Let them download:** Here's an opportunity for them to download white papers and other PDFs about your organization and products.
- **Encourage social sharing:** Embed Facebook, Twitter, and LinkedIn buttons so registrants can tweet or post that they just signed up for your webinar. Doing so promotes your event to a much wider audience. Over time, the additional viewers you capture via social sharing can add up to significant numbers.

Making Your Console Too Vanilla

If your console is too vanilla — you know, with a boring layout and few controls — maybe you're shortchanging your participant of the full experience. Think about it for a second — actually, think about it longer. After all, you're asking them to stare at a screen for an hour. If that location is not visually engaging, you will see them drop off quicker than flies around a bug lamp.

So what makes a great console? In the abstract, it's one that helps retain audience focus and attention throughout your presentation. But more specifically, it provides an opportunity to reinforce your branding and message. Remember, a well-designed console will engage your attendees and establish your brand.

TIP

To keep them interested, every console should include the following:

- **Your corporate logo and color scheme:** That should be clear to viewers from the start.
- **The presenter's top-line message at the top of the screen:** If attendees remember nothing else, they'll remember your key message after staring at it for an hour.
- **Appealing graphics:** Make the background of your webinar console visually appealing by using bold colors, images, and graphics. The console is your pallet upon which you overlay the audience experience.

Leaving the Audience Out of the Conversation

WARNING!

Your audience will never confide, "Honey, we don't talk anymore," but they will log off if they feel ignored. And it's a shame, because the ability to interact with your audience has become one of the most important developments in webinar technology. It's ridiculous to expect your attendees to stare at a screen watching a talking head, or worse looking at slides, for an hour. It's simply unacceptable. You have so many audience participation tools at your disposal. It's important to change the thought process from talking at your audience to having a conversation with them.

TIP

Here are a few ways to make them feel like part of the conversation:

- **Live Q&A:** The most widely used interactive tool in the webinar experience changes participants from being passive to active by allowing them to ask questions.
- **Polling:** Getting a feel from your audience by polling them during the webinar can be one of the most powerful tools in your arsenal. Not only does polling enable presenters to directly engage with viewers, but it also ensures they are paying attention by requiring them to take action. In addition, it allows attendees to benchmark themselves against their peers' votes. An added bonus is that you can gain interesting insights about your market or brand perception.

- **Social media:** Encourage your audience to use social media. When viewers can react to events in real time over social networks, it maintains engagement. That's why you should provide the tools to share directly from your console and keep them in your webinar.
- **Group chat:** By letting the audience communicate with one another, you expand the conversation by getting them to listen to you and their peers simultaneously.

Killing Your Audience with 1,000 Bullets (and Text too)

Asking your attendees for an hour of their time and attention is a lot to ask, but forcing them to stare at slides filled with endless text is sheer torture. It's the easiest way to drive people away from your webinar.

The bullet list goes down as one of the great presentation innovations, but unfortunately, overuse has dulled its appeal. After a few PowerPoint slides crammed with too many large dots preceding some words, your audience will start to tune out.

Since the days of the seminar in a hotel ballroom, presenters have struggled with the problem of excessive text, making the bullet list a great way to simplify things. But too many lists are just as unbearable as the excessive text that preceded them, making bullets more overplayed than Daft Punk's "Get Lucky." A bullet list is still a functional tool, but you need to rein it in.

Compelling slides combined with great storytelling is the key to keeping your audience's attention and getting your message across.

Consider the following:

- **Limit the amount of words you put on screen:** It distracts the audience from the host. Remember, the speaker is the storyteller, not the slide, so you want the audience concentrating on listening to what he has to say, rather than looking at the slide. If there's a need for lots of words, it's better for them to flow eloquently from the presenter's mouth.
- **You want to compel the audience with imagery, not word slides:** The best presentations tell compelling stories that are supported by engaging visuals.
- **A few bullets go a long way:** When using bullets, be sure they are not used in mind-numbing numbers and that they highlight key points. One idea is to summarize your words and pictures with a bullet list at the end of each section.

Selling Your Audience Out Instead of Helping Them

Don't get me wrong — it's okay to sell products via webinars. Just be upfront about it.

WARNING!

Aside from the occasional giggle, no one wants to sit and watch a snake-oil salesman do his thing, especially when an audience member registers for your webinar expecting to be helped. The looking-to-be-informed masses come to your presentation for answers to their pressing problems, or to consider new ideas. Now, what do you think happens when they realize they're just being pitched? That's right: They leave in droves. And that's sad because you are missing a valuable opportunity to establish credibility and earn trust.

Instead, you must offer prospective participants new ways to think about their toughest business problems. When you're direct and helpful, you establish yourself as a trusted advisor — a position that ultimately will enable you to more effectively present your solutions, products, or services.

Although your webinar should help them with topics such as "5 Keys to a Successful (insert name here)" or "How to Optimize (something)," it doesn't necessarily mean you can't address your product or service. Just do it from a perspective that helps solve their problem, rather than just making a sale.

WARNING!

Many companies conduct webinar product demonstrations, targeting serious buyers. These so-called "deminars" can be highly effective, but the audiences must know what they've signed up for. Don't pull a bait-and-switch. You know: Attract an audience with the promise of addressing a specific business problem but then give that problem a mere surface-level treatment before jumping right into a detailed product pitch. This tactic will backfire quicker than a 1978 Chevrolet Impala on a tank of bad gas. Plus, they won't trust you anymore and will delete your future e-mails.

Leaving Audio to Chance

Movies, television, and webinars all depend heavily on their visual aspect. Nothing turns off your audience more than terrible audio quality. If they can't hear your voice clearly, they can't hear your message.

That's because what we see on the screen is enhanced by how clearly we can hear it. Poor audio quality can frustrate audiences interested in your content, especially when they struggle to understand what's being said to them. They're busy, anyway, so guess what happens when they can't even hear your presentation? They drop out!

Audio is too important to leave to chance. When it's less than perfect, it can convey an air of unprofessionalism, which can lead to similar perceptions of your company as a whole. Webinar presenters should always use land lines with handsets or headsets because the audio quality is much better.

Consider the following to make sure your webinar sounds good and doesn't provide one more reason for your participant to drop out: Your audience will thank you by staying engaged with your webinar.

- **Never use cell phones or speaker phones:** The poor sound quality is evident.
- **Use a good-quality handset or headset:** The better sound quality is equally evident.
- **Do the presentation in a small room:** Big rooms often have an echo.
- **Turn off air conditioning, heaters, or other noisy devices:** You may think they can't be heard over the phone line, but you will discover that buzz or hum when it's too late.
- **Sound-check every speaker 30 minutes before the webinar:** This way, you have time to address any issues with audio quality in advance.

Dissing Your Audience's Time

Here's another way to alienate an audience: Don't respect your attendees' time. Some producers run their webinars past their end time, whereas others try to fill up the whole session by stretching the content. Avoid both.

Most webinars average 45–60 minutes in length; however, that does not mean that you should automatically schedule all of your events for that length. What if you only have 20 minutes of great content? Should you stretch it out? Probably not because you should never add filler — your audience can recognize it for what it is. Further, if your webinar is scheduled for one hour, make sure to stop when the hour is up. Respect the audience's time, and they will appreciate you more. Here are some points to remember:

- **Do not exceed the advertised webinar length:** When you run over, you're forcing the participant to make a decision that they don't want to make. Not only does it make you look unprofessional, you put them in the tough position of deciding between finishing your event or making it to their next meeting on time.
- **Schedule your webinar length based on your content:** Just because you have 60 minutes doesn't mean you should use the entire time, especially if your content doesn't support it. Determine how long it's going to take to make your presentation, and then add 10–15 minutes for Q&A. For example, if you need 30 minutes to present your content, include

15 minutes for Q&A, making it a 45-minute webinar. People know when they are getting filler and they'll drop off. Besides, a busy participant will appreciate the shorter time.

- **Start a tad late:** It's fairly standard practice to start webinars about two minutes after the hour to allow attendees running from another meeting to get to their computer, put on a headset, and log in. If you are running into unpreventable technical errors that are forcing you to start a little behind schedule, be sure your webinar moderator is keeping attendees completely in-the-know about what's going on and when your anticipated start time will be.
- **End a tad early:** If you still have five or ten minutes left in your allotted time but your presentation is complete and no more questions are coming in, don't be afraid to end your webinar early. Your audience won't think less of you — they will thank you and appreciate getting a few minutes back. In fact, this could earn you additional goodwill.

Following a "My Dog Ate My On-Demand" Strategy

It's hard to listen to a conversation about television without someone bringing up the DVR or TiVo, so it's pretty clear that we can't always make the appointment for our favorite TV show at its scheduled hour. So why would it be different when it comes to your webinar? That's why it's so important to have an on-demand strategy, so those who missed it can watch it later.

Studies show that one in four webinar registrants attends a webinar on-demand, and many of them miss the live event entirely. One reason is that most people don't have a lot of time during the day, so they are choosing to watch at "off" times, such as during long commutes. Also, remember that your webinar is accessible around the globe. The differing time zones of your attendees make it impossible for everyone to attend live. A global audience means your webinars have to be available on-demand for instant viewing at any time and on any type of device.

With on-demand viewing providing such a massive opportunity to extend the life of your webinar, it is important to have a plan to not only archive the event, but to promote it beyond the live date.

Consider the following:

- **Get it out quickly:** Be sure your webinars are available within 48 hours of the live event. The sooner you send out the link, the better.
- **Notify all registrants:** Let them know the archive link is available. Include everyone who attended, not just those who missed the webinar.

- **Be a gracious host:** That is, make sure to host the link to the archived content on your web site.
- **Share with your sales department:** Send them the link so they can promote it to their prospects.

Treating All Leads Equally

Although all men are created equal, all your leads are not. Prospects are the people you want to register for your webinar, but some clearly are more suited for your message than others. By tracking attendee activity and engagement, you can qualify leads. Unfortunately, many organizations have fallen into the habit of taking all the leads from a webinar and handing them over to the sales department without any pre-qualification.

This leads to sales reps working their way through more dead ends than you have in a fancy gated community. That's why it's important to assess each lead with the proper lead scoring. In this case, it refers to assigning leads to a ranking system that prioritizes interest in your topic. Most of the data you need on the attendees is already at your disposal from registration and their behavior during the webinar.

Intelligent lead scoring techniques allow you to evaluate and score leads based on criteria in two primary areas. By simply prioritizing the stronger leads, you will increase the effectiveness of your sales efforts and the *return on investment*, or ROI, of your webinars.

These include

- **Basic registration data:** From this information, you can quickly establish company size, industry, job title, and revenue, making it easy to qualify whether a prospect is right for you, and whether it makes sense for you to target the registrant further.
- **Behavioral data:** The increased level of interactivity in webinars not only serves to engage the audience, but it also provides a wealth of data on the interests of your attendees. This data can be combined to create an engagement score that provides you with the interest level of the prospect. This data can include viewing duration, content downloads, questions asked, poll/survey results, and social media engagement.

Index

• Number •

• A •

• B •

• C •

• D •

• E •

• N •

• O •

• P •

• Q •

• R •

• S •

• U •

• V •

• W •

• Y •

• Z •

About the Authors

John Carucci has written about photography and video for more than 20 years and has published four books on the subject: *Digital SLR Video and Filmmaking For Dummies* (John Wiley & Sons); *Nighttime Digital Photography with Photoshop CS3* (Peachpit); *The New Media Guide to Creative Photography* (Amphoto); and *Capturing the Night With Your Camera* (Amphoto).

Carucci has written more than one hundred articles on photography, video, and technology. His work has appeared in many publications including *American Photo*, *Popular Photography*, *PDN*, *Shutter Bug*, *Photo Pro*, *PC Photo*, and others. Carucci was also a contributing editor to *Popular Photography Magazine* from 2000–2002, writing about digital images and video technology. In addition, Carucci was contributing writer to *Photo Insider*, where he wrote a bi-monthly column called Digital Bytes from 1998 to 2002.

Currently, Carucci works as an entertainment news producer for Associated Press Television, where he covers music and theater. Those responsibilities include arranging and conducting studio interviews, covering field assignments (red carpets, news events, interviews, and so on), script writing, and editing both television packages and online segments. In addition to his television work, Carucci also writes general news stories on the entertainment beat. Prior to that appointment, he was a photo editor covering sports, national, international, and features.

Sharat Sharan

Sharat Sharan is cofounder and CEO of ON24 Inc., a global leader in webcasting and virtual environments with more than 1,000 customers. ON24 is the global market share leader in webcasting solutions. Sharan guided ON24 through multiple transitions, taking the company from an online financial news service for retail investors during the dot-com boom to a provider of webcasts and virtual events on the industry's leading virtual communications platform. Sharan was formerly vice president and general manager of Hearst New Media and Technology and vice president of the Hearst New Media Group. Prior to joining Hearst, Sharan was responsible for business development at AT&T Wireless Systems and a member of the AT&T Bell Laboratories technical staff. He holds an MBA from the University of Chicago and a master's degree in computer science from Virginia Tech.

Dedication

To my usual suspects on boats and stages!

— John Carucci

Author's Acknowledgments

It's not easy to pull off an entertaining and engaging webinar, and it's even harder to try and explain how to do it. This project was a true testament to how no man is an island. There are many people to thank, both those directly related to the project and those, well, directly related to me.

Let's start with the folks at Wiley, starting with executive editor Steve Hayes for continuing to provide challenges and having the patience to continually modify the plan to accommodate my busy schedule. Thanks to my editor, Linda Morris, for piecing these words and pictures together into a cohesive form.

I would also like to extend a great deal of gratitude to the folks at ON24. There's nothing like getting sound advice from the people that produce webinars on a grand stage on a regular basis. Special thanks to Tricia Heinrich, Christie Andersen, Mark Bornstein, Lars Christensen, Jackie Kiler, and Mark Szelenyi.

Thanks to my agent Carol Jelen for finding projects for me. I appreciate all your help.

And once again, thanks to Jillian, Anthony, and Alice for providing a base.

— John Carucci

Publisher's Acknowledgments

Executive Editor: Steve Hayes

Project Editor: Linda Morris

Copy Editor: Linda Morris

Editorial Assistant: Claire Johnson

Sr. Editorial Assistant: Cherie Case

Project Coordinator: Sheree Montgomery

Cover Image: © iStockphoto.com/Petar Chernaev

ISBN	Name	Author	Price
9788126533732	**Boosting Self-Esteem For Dummies**	Rhena Branch, Rob Willson	349.00
9788126533756	**Linkedin For Dummies, 2nd Edition**	Joel Elad	349.00
9788126533770	**Twitter Marketing For Dummies**	Kyle Lacy	349.00
9788126533589	**Job Searching With Social Media For Dummies**	Joshua Waldman	349.00
9788126533534	**Yoga For Dummies, 2nd Edition**	Georg Feuerstein, Larry Payne	399.00
9788126533565	**Work/Life Balance For Dummies**	Katherine Lockett, Jeni Mumford	349.00
9788126533541	**Facebook Marketing For Dummies, 2nd Edition**	Paul Dunay, Richard Krueger	349.00
9788126533725	**Leadership For Dummies**	Dr John Marrin	349.00
9788126533749	**Life Coaching For Dummies, 2nd Edition**	Jeni Purdie	349.00
9788126533688	**Professional Blogging For Dummies**	Susan J. Getgood	349.00
9788126533572	**Self-Hypnosis For Dummies**	Mike Bryant, Peter Mabbutt	349.00
9788126533558	**Social Media Marketing All-In-One For Dummies**	Jan Zimmerman, Doug Sahlin	499.00
9788126534661	**French For Dummies, 2nd Edition**	Dodi-Katrin Schmidt, Michelle M. Williams, Dominique Wenzel, Zoe Erotopoulos	399.00 w/CD
9788126534647	**German For Dummies, 2nd Edition**	Paulina Christensen, Anne Fox, Wendy Foster	399.00 w/CD
9788126534685	**Flirting For Dummies**	Elizabeth Clark	199.00
9788126534654	**Spanish For Dummies, 2nd Edition**	Susana Wald, Cecie Kraynak	399.00 w/CD
9788126534708	**Chinese For Dummies, Revised Edition**	Dr. Wendy Abraham	349.00 w/CD
9788126535873	**Dad's Guide To Pregnancy For Dummies**	Dr. Roger Henderson, Matthew M.F. Miller, Sharon Perkins	349.00
9788126535880	**Pregnancy For Dummies, 2nd Edition**	Dr. Sarah Jarvis, Dr Roger Henderson, Joanne Stone, Keith Eddleman, Mary Duenwald	349.00
9788126536498	**Confidence For Dummies, 2nd Edition**	Kate Burton, Brinley Platts	249.00
9788126536504	**Body Language For Dummies, 2nd Edition**	Elizabeth Kuhnke	349.00
9788126536511	**Excel 2010 For Dummies, Pocket Edition**	Greg Harvey	99.00
9788126536528	**Twitter For Dummies, Pocket Edition**	Laura Fitton, Michael E. Gruen, Leslie Poston	99.00
9788126538331	**Windows 8 For Dummies**	Andy Rathbone	349.00
9788126538744	**Meditation For Dummies, 3rd Edition**	Stephan Bodian	399.00
9788126538737	**Personal Branding For Dummies**	Susan Chritton	349.00
9788126538690	**Voice & Speaking Skills For Dummies**	Judy Apps	399.00
9788126538720	**Social Media Metrics For Dummies**	Leslie Poston	349.00
9788126538751	**Marketing For Dummies, 3rd Edition**	Ruth Mortimer, Greg Brooks, Craig Smith, Alexander Hiam	349.00
9788126538713	**Social Media Marketing For Dummies, 2nd Ed.**	Shiv Singh, Stephanie Diamond	349.00
9788126538768	**Performance Appraisals & Phrases For Dummies**	Ken Lloyd	199.00

ISBN	Name	Author	Price
9788126539109	**Social Media Marketing All-In-One For Dummies, 2nd Edition**	Jan Zimmerman, Deborah Ng	499.00
9788126538775	**Android Application Development For Dummies, 2nd Edition**	Michael Burton, Donn Felker	399.00
9788126538706	**Persuasion & Influence For Dummies**	Elizabeth Kuhnke	349.00
9788126539697	**Japanese For Dummies, 2nd Edition**	Eriko Sato	499.00 w/CD
9788126539093	**Six Sigma For Dummies, 2nd Edition**	Craig Gygi, Bruce Williams, Neil Decarlo	399.00
9788126539574	**Online Reputation Management For Dummies**	Lori Randall Stradtman	399.00
9788126541348	**Guitar For Dummies**	Mark Phillips, Jon Chappell	399.00 w/DVD
9788126541331	**Mind Mapping For Dummies**	Florian Rustler	399.00
9788126541355	**Success as a Mediator For Dummies**	Victoria Pynchon, Joe Kraynak	399.00
9788126541775	**Microsoft Excell 2013 All-in-One For Dummies**	Greg Harvey, Phd	499.00
9788126541751	**Microsoft Office 2013 All-in-One For Dummies**	Peter Weverka	499.00
9788126541768	**Microsoft Office 2013 For Dummies**	Wallace Wang	399.00
9788126542550	**Networking For Dummies, 10th Edition**	Lowe	399.00
9788126542567	**Excel Formulas and Functions For Dummies, 3rd Edition**	Bluttman	399.00
9788126542574	**Project Management For Dummies, 4th Edition**	Portny	399.00
9788126542475	**Critical Conversations For Dummies**	Schlachter	249.00
9788126542550	**Networking For Dummies**	Doug Lowe	399.00
9788126542574	**Project Management For Dummies**	Stanley E. Portny, PMP®	399.00
9788126542871	**Project 2013 For Dummies**	Cynthia snyder, Nancy Muir	449.00
9788126542918	**Hybrid Cloud For Dummies**	Judith Hurwitz, Marcia Kaufman Dr. Fern Halper, Daniel Kirsch	449.00
9788126543021	**Stress Management For Dummies**	Allen Elkin	399.00
9788126543014	**Mobile Marketing For Dummies**	Michael Becker, John Arnold	399.00
9788126542963	**Microsoft Office 2013 For Dummies with DVD Bundle**	Wallace Wang	599.00
9788126542970	**Microsoft Excel 2013 For Dummies with DVD Bundle**	Greg Harvey	599.00
9788126543281	**Big Data For Dummies**	Judith Hurwitz, Alan Nugent, Dr. Fern Halper, Marcia Kaufman	399.00
9788126543762	**Job Search Letters For Dummies**	Joyce Lain Kennedy	399.00
9788126543779	**Business Models For Dummies**	Jim Muehlhausen JD	399.00
9788126543786	**Hacking For Dummies, 4th Edition**	Kevin Beaver	399.00
9788126543793	**Business Analysis For Dummies**	Paul Mulvey, Kate McGoey, Kupe Kupersmith	449.00
9788126543809	**Psychology For Dummies, 2nd Edition**	Adam Cash	399.00
9788126543816	**Codependency For Dummies**	Darlene Lancer	399.00

ISBN	Name	Author	Price
9788126543977	**Competitive Intelligence For Dummies**	Jim Underwood	449.00
9788126544394	**Facebook For Dummies**	Carolyn Abram	399.00
9788126544387	**Neuromarketing For Dummies**	Stephen J. Genco, Andrew P. Pohlmann, Peter Steidl	499.00
9788126544776	**PMP Certification All-in-One For Dummies**	Cynthia Snyder	599.00
9788126544769	**Wine For Dummies, 5th Edition**	McCarthy, Mary Ewing-Mulligan	399.00
9788126544974	**Training Your Brain For Dummies**	Dr Tracy Packiam, Alloway	299.00
9788126544981	**Personal Development All-in-One For Dummies, 2nd Edition**	Edited by: Gillian Burn	499.00
9788126545346	**Counselling Skills For Dummies**	Gail Evans	399.00
9788126545353	**Passing Exam For Dummies**	Patrick Sherratt	299.00
9788126545810	**Data Driven Marketing For Dummies**	David Semmelroth	499.00
9788126545827	**Starting an Online Business For Dummies 7th Edition**	Greg Holden	499.00
9788126545964	**Java Programming For Android Developers For Dummies**	Barry Burd	449.00
9788126545971	**Social Collaboration For Dummies**	David F. Carr	449.00
9788126546183	**Oracle 12c For Dummies**	Chris Ruel, Michael Wessler	499.00
9788126546268	**Playing Keyboard For Dummies**	Jerry Kovarsky	499.00
9788126546442	**Success as an Introvert For Dummies**	Joan Pastor, PhD	399.00
9788126546640	**Blogging For Dummies 5th Edition**	Amy Lupold Bair, Susannah Gardner	499.00
9788126546657	**Business Storytelling For Dummies**	Karen Dietz, PhD, Lori L. Silverman	499.00
9788126524877	**Cloud Computing For Dummies**	Judith Hurwitz, Robin Bloor, Marcia Kaufman, Fern Halper	499.00
9788126547128	**Networking All-in-One For Dummies 5th Ed.**	Doug Lowe	599.00
9788126547548	**Russian For Dummies**	Andrew Kaufman, PhD, and Serafima Gettys, PhD	499.00 w/CD
9788126547555	**Arabic For Dummies**	Amine Bouchentouf	499.00 w/CD
9788126548590	**Visual Social Marketing For Dummies**	Krista Neher	499.00
9788126548972	**Java All-in-One For Dummies 4th Edition**	Doug Lowe	599.00
9788126548965	**Predictive Analytics For Dummies**	Anasse Bari,PhD, Mohamed Chaouchi, Tommy Jung	549.00
9788126549177	**Excel Dashboards & Reports For Dummies®, 2nd Edition**	Michael Alexander	449.00
9788126549184	**Lead Generation For Dummies**	Dayna Rothman	449.00
9788126549276	**3D Printing For Dummies**	Kalani Kirk Hausman Richard Horne	499.00
9788126549467	**Hinduism For Dummies**	Dr. Amrutur V. Srinivasan	499.00
9788126550449	**Mindfulness at Work For Dummies**	Shamash Alidina and Juliet Adams	499.00

ISBN	Name	Author	Price	
9788126550418	**Salesforce.com For Dummies 5th Edition**	Liz Kao and Matt Kaufman	499.00	
9788126550432	**Marketing Automation For Dummies**	Mathew Sweezey	499.00	
9788126550425	**Piano & Keyboard All-in-One For Dummies**	Holly Day, Jerry Kovarsky, Blake Neely, David Pearl, and Michael Pilhofer	599.00	
9788126550470	**Running Great Meetings & Workshops For Dummies**	Jessica Pryce-Jones Julia Lindsay	299.00	
9788126550487	**Business Networking For Dummies**	Stefan Thomas	299.00	
9788126550500	**Facebook All-in-One For Dummies, 2nd Edition**	Jamie Crager, Scott Ayres, Melanie Nelson, and Daniel Herndon	599.00	
9788126550517	**Hadoop For Dummies**	Dirk deRoos, Paul c. Zikopoulos, Roman B. Melnyk, PhD Bruce Brown Rafael Coss	499.00	
9788126550524	**Excel Data Analysis For Dummies, 2nd Edition**	Stephen L. Nelson	499.00	
9788126550531	**Beginning iOS Programming For Dummies**	Rajiv Ramnath, PhD	499.00	
9788126550548	**iOS App Development For Dummies**	Jesse Feiler	499.00	
9788126551002	**Lean Six Sigma for Dummies, 2nd Edition**	John Morgan, Martin Brening-Jones	499.00	
9788126551286	**Social Media Design For Dummies**	Janine Warner and David LaFontaine	499.00	
9788126551279	**Innovative Presentations For Dummies**	Ray Anthony and Barbara Boyd	449.00	
9788126552016	**R For Dummies**	Andrie de Vries Joris Meys	499.00	
9788126552184	**Windows 8.1 For Dummies**	Andy Rathbone	449.00	
9788126552191	**Willpower For Dummies**	Frank Ryan	149.00	
9788126552252	**UX For Dummies**	Donald Chesnut, Kevin P. Nichols	499.00	
9788126552269	**Lean Six Sigma Business Transformation For Dummies**	Roger Burghall, Vince Grant & John Morgan	499.00	
9788126552290	**Facebook Marketing For Dummies, 4th Edition**	John Haydon	499.00	
9788126552306	**Chinese For Dummies, 2nd Edition**	Wendy Abraham	499.00	w/CD
9788126552801	**Webinars For Dummies**	John Carucci & Sharat Sharan	499.00	
9788126552818	**Guitar All-In-One For Dummies, 2nd Edition**	Jon chappell, Mark Phillips, and Desi Serna	599.00	
9788126552825	**Beginning Programming with Java For Dummies**	Barry Burd, PhD	499.00	

Available wherever books are sold. For more information or to order direct: U.S. customers visit www.dummies.com or call 1-877-762-2974. U.K. customers visit www.wileyeurope.com or call (0) 1243 843291. canadian customers visit www.wiley.ca or call 1-800-567-4797.

Connect with us online at www.facebook.com/fordummies or @fordummies